CURIOUS

Ian Leslie lives in London where he combines careers in advertising and writing. His book *Born Liars: Why We Can't Live Without Deceit* was hailed as 'consistently startling and fascinating' by the Daily Mail and was BBC Radio 4's 'Book of the Week'. He writes about ideas, culture, and politics for a wide range of publications including *Intelligent Life*, the *New Statesman*, and the *Guardian*, and is the creator and presenter of the BBC radio comedy, *Before They Were Famous*.

'An inspiring read that gives lie to the old saying that ignorance is bliss'   *Good Book Guide*

'A lovely, erudite exploration of what it is that makes us human'   *Independent on Sunday*

'Timely and readable'   *Guardian*

'Leslie . . . writes convincingly . . . about the human need and desire to learn deeply and develop expertise'
Wall Street Journal

'Stuffed with facts, ide̶   ̶ind-
ings, puzzles, mysterie̶   — as
Montaigne said of trav̶   lish"
one's brain. It's the most delightful ̶   about
the mind in quite some time'   *New York Times*

IAN LESLIE

CURIOUS

The
DESIRE
to Know
& Why
Your
FUTURE
Depends
on it

Quercus

First published in Great Britain in 2014 by
Quercus Editions Ltd

This edition published in 2015 by

Quercus Publishing Ltd
Carmelite House
50 Victoria Embankment
London EC4Y 0DZ

An Hachette UK company

A CIP catalogue record for this book is available from the British Library

ISBN PB 978 1 78206 497 8
ISBN EBook 978 1 78206 496 1

Text designed and typeset by Ellipsis Digital Limited, Glasgow

Printed and bound in Great Britain by Clays Ltd, St Ives plc

For Io: may she never stop getting excited
by what she doesn't yet know

I have no special talents. I am only passionately curious.

Albert Einstein

I mean that if it is important for us to eat first of all, it is even more important for us not to waste in the sole concern for eating our simple power of being hungry.

Antonin Artaud

Curiosity is insubordination in its purest form.

Vladimir Nabokov

Contents

PART THREE: STAYING CURIOUS

INTRODUCTION
The Fourth Drive

The researchers first realised that Kanzi was an unusually talented ape when they discovered that he had taught himself language.

Sue Savage-Rumbaugh and her colleagues at the Language Research Center near Atlanta, Georgia, had devoted months of painstaking effort to teaching Kanzi's adoptive mother, Matata, how to communicate using symbols. They worked with a keyboard that had lexigrams corresponding to things and actions in the real world; there was a key for apple, another one for play.

Despite being exceptionally intelligent, Matata made slow progress. She understood that the keyboard could be used to communicate, but the idea that specific symbols had specific significance eluded her. She would take Savage-Rumbaugh's hand and lead her to the keyboard, intent on sharing what was on her mind. Then Matata would press any key and look up expectantly, as if Savage-Rumbaugh would surely know what she meant. She might press 'juice' when what she really wanted was a banana, or 'groom' when she wanted to go outdoors.

While the researchers were working with Matata, Kanzi was usually in the room, entertaining himself. It had been a condition of Kanzi's transfer to the Language Center at six months old that he be allowed to remain with his mother while she participated in language studies. A hyperactive infant, Kanzi darted around the test room, jumping on his mother's head, pushing her hand away from the keyboard just as she was trying to hit a key, stealing the food she earned as a reward for good work.

The researchers had noticed that Kanzi also liked to play with the keyboard when it was free, but they thought little of it. Then one day, when he was two years old, Kanzi went up to the keyboard and very deliberately selected the 'chase' key. He looked at Savage-Rumbaugh to see if she had noticed what he'd done. When she nodded and smiled, he ran off, looking behind him as he did so, a big, cheeky grin on his face.

That day, Kanzi used the keyboard 120 times, making requests for specific foods or games, or announcing what he was about to do. To the astonishment of Savage-Rumbaugh and her colleagues, it became clear that he had mastered the symbolic keyboard, despite having never been trained on it, or even seeming to have paid attention to his mother's lessons. Over the following months and years the researchers turned their full attention to this ape prodigy. Kanzi went on to demonstrate linguistic aptitude of such sophistication that he changed the way cognitive psychologists thought about human learning and language.

The difference between an ape and a human being is less than you might think. Kanzi learned a vocabulary of over 200 words. When he was given tests of reading and communications skills he matched, and in some respects excelled, a child of two and a half years old. He made up and follows his own rules of grammar, indicating a creative capacity. He understands spoken language and can follow spoken instructions – when Savage-Rumbaugh told him to throw something into the river, he picked up a rock and hurled it in. He can use symbols to ask for treats, or for help opening a door. He loves to play, and he loves to learn.

The story of Kanzi shows just how much we have in common with apes, which ought not to be a surprise, given that we share nearly all of their DNA. Yet it also suggests there is something that isn't shared – something very important.

What Kanzi never did, and never does, is ask *why*. He never furrows his brow, leans over the keyboard and bashes out a sentence like, 'Why are you asking me all these questions?' or 'What *exactly* are you trying to discover?' He doesn't ask about what lies beyond the confines of his home at the research centre. He can go to the refrigerator, but he has no interest in how the refrigerator works. Although he spends time with human beings who are clearly interested in what it is like to be an ape, Kanzi shows no curiosity about what it's like to be human. For that matter, he shows little curiosity in what it means to be an ape. He has never asked, 'Who am I?'

'Who am I?' was the question to which John Lloyd awoke on the morning of Christmas Eve, 1993. It didn't come to him in the form of a dreamy, philosophical rumination. It was urgent, painful, and insistent. It felt like a drill to the head.

Lloyd hadn't lost his memory. He could answer his question in all the ways you would expect. 'I'm John Lloyd. I'm forty-two years old. I'm 6'1. I'm a successful TV producer and director. I have homes in London and Oxfordshire. I'm married, with three children.' But, that morning, none of these answers did anything to salve the pain of the inquiry. The more he thought about it, the more he felt his question pointed not to a loss, but a lack. 'I realised,' he later told me, 'that I didn't *know* anything.'

Of course, Lloyd did know things. He knew a lot about how to make commercials. He also knew something about how to make TV comedy. During the preceding decade and a half – or as he described it to me, 'fifteen insane years' – he had gone on an extraordinary, unprecedented hot streak of success, producing some of the most popular and loved comedy shows in Britain, including *Not the Nine O'Clock News*, *Blackadder* and *Spitting Image*.

Lloyd was instrumental in the early successes of some of Britain's most famous actors and comedians, including Rowan Atkinson, Richard Curtis, Stephen Fry and Hugh

Laurie. He had won numerous BAFTAs – Britain's Oscars – for those shows, and for his advertising campaigns. In fact, as he told me, with a mixture of pride and sheepishness, 'I've won more BAFTAs than anyone except Dame Judi Dench.' He was given a Lifetime Achievement Award before he was forty.

Shortly afterwards, things started going wrong. Lloyd's flawless career hit serious snags. He was fired from advertising campaigns he had created. The head of a Hollywood studio threw his movie script into a swimming pool. Nothing he tried to start got off the ground. He had dealt with disappointments before, but this was different. His failures were as relentless as his previous success had seemed unstoppable. It felt like he was being bullied by a giant bear: 'Every time I tried to pick myself up, I was smacked down again.'

That Christmas Eve, Lloyd had been shaken awake by the horrifying thought that everything he had done or achieved thus far was worthless. The BAFTAs on his shelves turned to cardboard. Lloyd entered a serious depression, despite knowing that he had much to be thankful for. Nevertheless, in the years that followed, an intruder to the Lloyd home might have come across the most successful TV producer of his generation sitting under his desk, crying.

Lloyd decided to deal with his depression with the same determination with which he had once set about persuading the BBC to recommission a failed sitcom set in medieval England called *Blackadder*. He eschewed some of the popular strategies for coping with male mid-life crises: he didn't go into therapy, buy a sports car or leave his wife. Instead, he took time off work, went on long walks, and drank whisky. He also started to read. 'I didn't read any book during those years of success. I never had time.' Despite attending one of Britain's top schools and graduating from Cambridge, Lloyd never considered himself particularly knowledgeable. Now he had the time to catch up.

He read about Socrates and ancient Athens. He read about light and magnetism. He read about the Renaissance, and the French Impressionists. He had no method or plan, but simply followed his curiosity, wherever it took him. On coming across, for the first time, Caillebotte's painting of workmen varnishing a Parisian floor, Lloyd grew interested in the history of varnish and found books to read about that. When he started making ads again, he would take a pile of books with him on the plane to far-flung locations, and devour their contents. The more he learned, the more he wanted to learn.

He was appalled at how little he knew, and intimidated by how much there was to catch up on. He was also furious that no one had thought to let him in on a secret: 'I was suddenly seeing that the world is incredibly *interesting*. If you're paying attention, everything in the world – from the nature of gravity, to a pigeon's head, to a blade of grass – is extraordinary.' School had been a chore, dull but necessary. This was a pleasure, verging on an obsession. 'The closer you look at anything, the more interesting it gets. But nobody *tells* you this.'

Underpinning his fascination with everything was a driving desire to understand nothing less than the meaning of life. 'I was really trying to find out, what is the point of me? What is the point of anything?'

Six years after he had embarked on his meandering journey through the world's store of knowledge, Lloyd, now over the worst of his depression, was standing in the study of his Oxfordshire home, surrounded by books when, 'Suddenly the top of my head opened, and I thought, hang on. Here's an idea: *QI*.' He saw how what had obsessed him for the last few years could be turned into entertainment. 'It will be a programme about interesting things. It will prove that everything is *quite interesting* if you look at it from the right angle.'

QI became a BBC quiz show, hosted by Stephen Fry. It is now one of Britain's most popular and long-running TV series, loved by millions for its ability to make anything — from quantum physics to Aztec architecture — entertaining and, well, interesting. The format is popular abroad, and the book version sells in the hundreds of thousands. Lloyd had finally scored another success, and he was prouder of this one than any of his others: 'It was the idea of my life.'

When Lloyd was pitching *QI* to the BBC, he and his team explained its underlying philosophy to the assembled executives. 'There is nothing more important or more strange than curiosity,' Lloyd told them. Ever since Darwin, he said, we have had to come to terms with the fact that we share with our primate cousins the same three basic drives: food, sex and shelter. But humans possess something else: a fourth drive. 'Pure curiosity is unique to human beings. When animals snuffle around in bushes it's because they're looking for the three other things. It's only people, as far as we know, who look up at the stars and wonder what they are.'

Our oldest stories about curiosity are warnings: Adam and Eve and the apple of knowledge, Icarus and the sun, Pandora's box. Early Christian theologians railed against curiosity: St Augustine claimed that 'God fashioned hell for the inquisitive'. Even the humanist philosopher Erasmus suggested that curiosity was greed by a different name. For most of Western history, it has been regarded as, at best, a distraction, at worst a poison, corrosive to the soul and to society.

There's a reason for this. Curiosity is unruly. It doesn't like rules, or at least, it assumes that all rules are provisional, subject to the laceration of a smart question nobody has yet thought to ask. It disdains the approved pathways, preferring diversions, unplanned excursions, impulsive left turns. In short, curiosity is deviant. Pursuing it is liable to bring you into conflict with authority at some point, as everyone from Galileo to Charles Darwin to Steve Jobs could have attested.

A society that values order above all else will seek to suppress curiosity. But a society that believes in progress, innovation and creativity will cultivate it, recognising that the enquiring minds of its people constitute its most valuable asset. In medieval Europe, the enquiring mind – especially if it enquired too closely into the edicts of Church or state — was stigmatised. During the Renaissance and Reformation, received wisdoms began to be interrogated, and by the time of the Enlightenment, European societies started to see that their future lay with the curious, and encouraged probing questions rather than stamping on them. The result was the biggest explosion of new ideas and scientific advances in history.

The great unlocking of curiosity translated into a cascade of prosperity for the nations that precipitated it. Today, we cannot know for sure if we are in the middle of this golden period or at the end of it. But we are, at the very least, in a lull. With the important exception of the internet, the innovations that catapulted Western societies ahead of the global pack are thin on the ground, while the rapid growth of Asian and South American economies has not yet been accompanied by a comparable run of indigenous innovation. Tyler Cowen, a professor of economics at George Mason University in Virginia, has termed the current period 'the great stagnation'.

Cowen says that the rich world is struggling to cope with the consequences of its own success; it now finds it much harder to raise the education levels of its populaces. Rather than just getting more people to school and university, therefore, the new challenge is to find ways of making more people hungry to learn, question and create. Meanwhile, the leaders of Asian societies, like those of China and Singapore, are wondering how to instil a culture of enquiry and critical thinking into their education systems, aware that people who defer too much to the authority of their elders' ideas are less likely to transcend them. The world is in need of more curious learners.

Edmund Phelps, the Nobel Prize-winning economist, believes that the grassroots spirit of enterprise which fuelled the Industrial Revolution is being suffocated by the dead weight of state and corporate bureaucracies. During a round-table discussion of his work, a senior executive at the international bank BNY Mellon told Phelps:

> So much of what you've talked about is what we struggle with daily as a large global financial corporation ... as our regulators and societies want us to be more controlled, we want to create a culture that is more collaborative, is more creative and more competitive. We need our staff to be active, enquiring, imaginative, and full of ideas and curiosity in order to create innovation.

The truly curious will be increasingly in demand. Employers are looking for people who can do more than follow procedures competently or respond to requests; who have a strong intrinsic desire to learn, solve problems and ask penetrating questions. They may be difficult to manage at times, these individuals, for their interests and enthusiasms can take them along unpredictable paths, and they don't respond well to being told what to think. But for the most part, they will be worth the difficulty.

The Fourth Drive

Curious learners go deep, and they go wide. They are the people best equipped for the kind of knowledge-rich, cognitively challenging work required in industries like finance or software engineering. They are also the ones most likely to make creative connections *between* different fields, of the kind that leads to new ideas, and the ones best suited to working in multi-disciplinary teams. Consequently, they are the ones whose jobs are least likely to be taken by intelligent machines; in a world where technology is rapidly replacing humans even in white-collar jobs, it's no longer enough to be merely smart. Computers are smart. But no computer, however sophisticated, can yet be said to be curious.

Another way of putting this is that there is a rising premium on people with a high 'need for cognition'. Need for cognition, or NFC, is a scientific measure of intellectual curiosity. The drive to make sense of the world is a universal characteristic of human beings, but the world is divided into those who always seek out short cuts, and those who prefer to take the scenic route. Psychologists use a scale of NFC to distinguish between individuals who like their mental life to be as straightforward as possible, and those who derive satisfaction and pleasure from intellectual challenges.

I'm going to assume that if you're reading this book you have a reasonably high NFC, but here is a simple way to assess yourself, based on a questionnaire invented by the psychologists who first formulated the concept. Answer each question 'true' or 'false', choosing the answer that most often applies to you (truthfully!):

11

CURIOUS

1. I would prefer complex to simple problems.
2. I like to have the responsibility of handling a situation that requires a lot of thinking.
3. Thinking is not my idea of fun.
4. I would rather do something that requires little thought than something that is sure to challenge my thinking abilities.
5. I try to anticipate and avoid situations where there is likely chance I will have to think in depth about something.
6. I find satisfaction in deliberating hard and for long hours.
7. I only think as hard as I have to.
8. I prefer to think about small, daily projects to long-term ones.
9. I like tasks that require little thought once I've learned them.
10. The idea of relying on thought to make my way to the top appeals to me.
11. I really enjoy a task that involves coming up with new solutions to problems.
12. Learning new ways to think doesn't excite me very much.
13. I prefer my life to be filled with puzzles that I can't solve.
14. The notion of thinking abstractly is appealing to me.
15. I would prefer a task that is intellectual, difficult and

important to one that is somewhat important but does
not require much thought.
16. I feel relief rather than satisfaction after completing
a task that required a lot of mental effort.
17. It's enough for me that something gets the job done.
I don't care how or why it works.
18. I usually end up deliberating about issues even when
they do not affect me personally.

If you answered 'true' to most of the questions 1, 2, 6, 10,
11, 13, 14, 15 and 18 and 'false' to most of the others then
the chances are you are higher in NFC than the average
person.

People who are low in NFC are more likely to rely on
others to explain things, or to fall back on cognitive heu-
ristics, like agreeing with what everyone else seems to be
saying. If you are high in NFC, you are more likely to
actively seek out experiences and information that make you
think, challenge your assumptions, and pose puzzles. You
have a restless, enquiring mind, and you are constantly on
the lookout for new intellectual journeys. Low NFC people
are 'cognitive misers' who seek to expend as little mental
effort as they can get away with, whereas high NFC people
positively enjoy 'effortful cognitive activity' – they are the
ones who read non-fiction books like this one, or tingle with
anticipation at the prospect of learning about a new idea.

That word 'effortful' is important – a major concern
of this book is that digital technologies are severing the

link between effort and mental exploration. By making it easier for us to find answers, the web threatens habits of deeper enquiry – habits that require patience and focused application. When you're confident that you can find out anything you want on your smartphone, you may be less likely to make the effort to learn the kind of knowledge that might lead you to query the answer that comes top of a Google search. As we'll see, there are those who argue that by releasing us of the need to use our memories, the internet is allowing us to be more creative. But such claims fly in the face of everything scientists have learned about how the mind works.

Effort and pleasure can go together, of course. If you are high in NFC, you are probably good at solving problems for your employer, because you're really solving them for yourself. Social scientists who study group behaviour have observed a phenomenon they call 'social loafing' – the widespread tendency of individuals to decrease their own effort when they start working collaboratively. When confident that others are working on the same problem, most people cut themselves some slack. But individuals who are high in need for cognition seem to form an exception to this rule; when given a cognitively challenging task to do in a group, they generate just as many different ideas as when working alone. They're having fun.

If you scored high on the test, congratulations. Don't let it go to your head, though. Just because you have a high NFC now, doesn't mean you'll always have one – as John

Lloyd can tell you. It's true that some people are more disposed to be cognitively demanding of themselves than others. But the scientific literature on curiosity, while it disagrees on many things, agrees on this: a person's curiosity is more state than trait. That is, our curiosity is highly responsive to the situation or environment we're in. It follows that we can arrange our lives to stoke our curiosity or squash it.

Curiosity is vulnerable to benign neglect. As we grow older we tend to become less active explorers of our mental environment, relying on what we've learned so far to see us through the rest of the journey. We can also become too preoccupied with the daily skirmishes of existence to take the time to pursue our interests. If you allow yourself to become incurious, your life will be drained of colour, interest and pleasure. You will be less likely to achieve your potential at work or in your creative life. While barely noticing it, you'll become a little duller, a little dimmer. You may not think it could happen to you, but it can. It can happen to any of us. To stop it happening, you need to understand what feeds curiosity, and what starves it.

That's what this book is about.

Sometime in the early 1480s, Leonardo da Vinci made a doodle in his notebook. He seems to have bought a new pen and was trying it out, absent-mindedly. What he wrote was a wandering riff on the phrase '*Dimmi*' ('Tell me'). 'Tell me . . . tell me whether . . . tell me how things are . . .'

Curiosity starts with the itch to explore. From a very early age, we display a yearning to conquer the unknown. A 1964 study found that babies as young as two months old, when presented with different patterns, will show a marked preference for the unfamiliar ones. Every parent knows about the child's compulsion to stick tiny fingers where they are not supposed to go, to run out of the open door, to eat dirt. This attraction to everything novel is what the scientists who study it call *diversive* curiosity.

In adults, diversive curiosity manifests itself as a restless desire for the new and the next. The modern world seems designed to stimulate our diversive curiosity. Every tweet, headline, ad, blog post and app at once promises and denies a satisfaction for which we are ever more impatient. Our popular entertainments are expertly crafted to hook our attention and keep it, by moving fast; the average shot in an American movie today is about two seconds, compared with 27.9 seconds in 1953.

Diversive curiosity is essential to an exploring mind; it opens our eyes to the new and undiscovered, encouraging us to seek out new experiences and meet new people. But unless it's allowed to deepen and mature it can become a futile waste of energy and time, dragging us from one object of attention to another without reaping insight from any. Unfettered curiosity is wonderful; unchannelled curiosity is not. When diversive curiosity is entrained – when it is transformed into a quest for knowledge and understanding – it nourishes us. This deeper, more disciplined and effortful type of curiosity is called *epistemic* curiosity, and it is the chief subject of this book.[*]

For individuals, epistemic curiosity can be a font of satisfaction and delight that provides sustenance for the soul. For organisations and nations it can supercharge creative talent and ignite innovation, turning the base metal of diversive curiosity into gold. To get a probe to Mars you need a powerful desire to explore a distant planet, but you will need to combine this with an enduring appetite for problem solving if you are to figure out how to get a camera up there.

Diversive curiosity has always been with us, and so has epistemic curiosity, but the latter has only flourished on a widespread scale in the modern era, since the invention of the printing press allowed people to read, share and combine ideas from all over the world, and since the Industrial Revolution created more time for more people to think and experiment. The internet ought to be giving epistemic curiosity another epochal boost, because it is making knowledge more widely available than ever before. But its amazing potential is undermined by our tendency to use it merely to stimulate diversive curiosity.

A secondary subject of this book is *empathic* curiosity:

---

[*] Curiosity is often discussed in relation to scientific discovery. Science and scientists certainly play major roles in this book. But I'll be placing curiosity in a wider context, one that accommodates curiosity about the structure of a Beethoven symphony or the life of Martin Luther King. Epistemic curiosity, in these pages, refers to a wide-ranging desire for intellectual and cultural exploration.

curiosity about the thoughts and feelings of other people. Empathic curiosity is distinct from gossip or prurience, which we can think of as diversive curiosity about the superficial detail of others' lives. You practise empathic curiosity when you genuinely try to put yourself in the shoes — and the mind — of the person you're talking to; to see things from their perspective. Diversive curiosity might make you wonder what a person does for a living; empathic curiosity makes you wonder *why* they do it. I'll be arguing that empathic curiosity became a common cognitive habit at around the same point in history as epistemic curiosity.

It is no coincidence that the two are tied to each other; curiosity is a deeply social quality. Almost from the beginning of life, we wonder about what it is that other people know that we don't; a baby's way of saying 'tell me' is to point to an object while looking at her mother. Whether our curiosity grows or shrinks is also dependent on others. If the baby's mother answers his wordless question he'll point to something else. If she ignores his gesture, he'll stop pointing. It's a dynamic that works its way through our lives, from home to school to the office. Curiosity is contagious. So is incuriosity.

Our attitudes to curiosity retain the taint of ancient warnings. We call people 'curious' when we mean 'weird'. We associate intellectual curiosity with dusty academics immersed in esoterica, or with the lone eccentric tinkering in his study, rather than with innovation, collaboration or entrepreneurialism. Curiosity is regarded by companies and governments as, at worst, a threat to established orders, and at best, a wasteful luxury.

As a result, we fail to invest in it. Our education system is increasingly focused on preparing students for specific jobs. To teach someone to be an engineer or a lawyer or a programmer is not the same as teaching them to be a curious learner – and yet the people who make the best engineers, lawyers and programmers tend to be the most curious learners. So we find ourselves stuck in a self-defeating cycle: we ask schools to focus on preparing students for the world of work, rather than on inspiring them, and we end up with uninspired students and mediocre professionals. The more we chase the goal of efficient education, the further it recedes.

The rewards of curiosity have never been higher, but our ideas about how curiosity works are muddled and misguided. We romanticise the natural curiosity of children and worry that it will be contaminated by knowledge, when the opposite is true. We confuse the practice of curiosity with ease of access to information, and forget that real curiosity requires the exercise of effort. We focus on the goals of learning rather than valuing learning for itself. Epistemic curiosity is in danger of becoming the province of cognitive elites, with far too many of us losing or never learning the capacity to think deeply about a subject or a person. In a world where vast inequalities in access to information are finally being levelled, a new divide is emerging – between the curious and the incurious.

The only reason people do not know much is because they do not care much. They are incurious. Incuriosity is the oddest and most foolish failing there is.

Stephen Fry

The most fundamental reason to choose curiosity isn't so that we can do better at school or at work. The true beauty of learning stuff, including apparently useless stuff, is that it takes us out of ourselves, reminds us that we are part of a far greater project, one that has been underway for at least as long as human beings have been talking to each other. Other animals don't share or store their knowledge like we do. Orangutans do not reflect on the history of the orangutan; London's pigeons have not adopted ideas on navigation from pigeons in Rio de Janeiro. We should all feel privileged to have access to a deep well of species memory. As Stephen Fry suggests, it's foolish not to take advantage of it.

Yet that's how many people live. I went to a school where few pupils read books unless they had to. Most of my school friends left school at the earliest legal opportunity. University was a soft option – a way of deferring adulthood. Being a man (I went to a boys' school) meant getting a job, putting learning behind you. I never felt like that, in large part because my parents, neither of whom attended university, infected me with their curiosity about the world. They had hungry minds, and the shelves at home were full of books, bought not for the purpose of decoration but enjoyment and edification. Conversations around the dinner table were as likely to be about history, music or politics as what we'd done that day. Being epistemically curious seemed like a natural way of life. As I grew older I came to think of it as a crucial condition of feeling fulfilled and alive.

Science supports this intuition. Neurologists use the term 'cognitive reserve' to describe the brain's capacity to resist the ravages of old age. For a study published in 2013, a team led by Robert Wilson at the Rush University Medical Centre in Chicago enrolled 300 elderly people, and tested their thinking and memory skills each year. The participants were also asked about how often they read, wrote and engaged in other cognitively demanding activities, not just currently, but in childhood and middle age. Following each participant's death, their brain was examined for evidence of dementia. It was discovered that, after taking the physical effects of dementia on their brains into account, the subjects who made a lifelong habit of lots of reading and writing slowed their rate of mental decline by *a third* compared to those who did only an average amount of those things.* In other words, these people had cheated old age. Years spent in intellectual pursuits meant they had accrued extra neuronal capacity, buffering them against the debilitating effects of

---

* People who rarely read or wrote experienced a decline that was a staggering forty-eight per cent faster compared to the average participants.

age. A lifelong investment in their cognitive reserve was paying back.

We are part biological organism, part cultural; we need both sunlight and knowledge to thrive. While I was writing this book I became a father for the first time, to a little girl. As I watch her hungry eyes attempt to penetrate the mysterious world in which she finds herself – the studiousness with which she examines her own toes! – I can feel the urgent pulse of her desire to know. I hope it never fades; I hate to think it will. After researching this book, I realise that's up to me as well as her.

John Lloyd told me how he came to see that during the years of his greatest successes, he wasn't fully human. 'If human curiosity isn't fed then you die inside,' he told me. 'A quarter of your desire to be alive is cut away.' At least that, I'd say.

'Beyond the age of information,' said the designer Charles Eames, 'is the age of choices.' Isn't it time to reassess your relationship with what Aristotle called 'the desire to know' – to *choose* curiosity?

PART 1
HOW CURIOSITY WORKS

CHAPTER 1

Three Journeys

In the 1960s Brian Smith was growing up in an apartment over a shoe store in a poor but lively neighbourhood of St Louis, Missouri. The part of town in which his family lived was crowded and busy, full of cars, restaurants, bars and nightclubs. In the evenings, the red light of a neon sign for Red Goose Shoes shone through the window into their living room.

One evening when he was about ten years old, Brian and his younger brother Paul were playing in their parents' bedroom. They started rummaging through the dresser drawers. While doing so they came across a large, solid object tucked under their father's underwear. Lifting up the clothes, they discovered what it was: a gun. The brothers were transfixed. They let themselves touch its cold metallic surface, feeling little shock waves of excitement travel up their arms.

Brian picked the gun up. It was unexpectedly heavy. Holding the weapon's muzzle towards his face, he could see that its cylinder was loaded with bullets. The brothers were fans of TV programmes like *The Lone Ranger* and *The Cisco Kid*, and in their parents' bedroom that day they staged pretend gunfights. One brother would take turns to point the weapon at the other, who would then take the shot, falling dramatically to the ground. Then they put the gun back in the drawer, being careful to replace it under the clothes, exactly as it had been found.

For weeks after that, the gun in the drawer was the boys' secret, one they vowed not to share with anyone else. Then one evening, Brian and his siblings (there were four in all) found themselves alone in the house for a short period. Brian was watching TV in his parents' bedroom. It was a warm evening and the window was open. Though he tried not to, Brian kept thinking about the gun, just a few feet away. In the end, he recalls, 'My curiosity got the better of me.'

Brian went to the dresser, retrieved the gun from the drawer, and walked over to the open window. Pretending to be an assassin, he pointed the weapon at the people walking along the sidewalk opposite his apartment on their way to a bar or restaurant for the evening. He imagined pulling the trigger, and simulated a recoil gesture, just like the ones he had seen people make on TV when they fired a shot. He dared to cock back the hammer of the gun, thrilling to the sound of its *click*. He took aim at the Red Goose sign, resting his finger lightly on the trigger. Then something happened.

BOOM! The red neon goose suddenly went dark. Disoriented, Brian saw smoke coming from the muzzle of the revolver. He looked out of the window. Down on the sidewalk, pedestrians were scrambling for cover and trying to work out where the shot had come from. Brian ducked out of sight. He replaced the gun in his parents' dresser drawer, and sat back down in front of the TV, his heart racing. *What the hell just happened*? He was terrified that he had shot someone.

His brother came into the room. 'What was that big bang?' 'I don't know,' said Brian, eyes on the TV, heart hammering. When his brother had gone, he took a surreptitious glance out of the window. He couldn't see any bodies in the street. His mother came home complaining about some idiot having fired a gun outside, but she didn't mention any casualties. No ambulance sirens sounded. The cars and pedestrians resumed their flow, Brian's heart gradually resumed its normal rate.

Brian and his brother were lucky, as were the pedestrians who nearly got in the way of the bullet Brian fired that day. In 2013, a nine-year-old boy in Decatur, Ohio was playing with a loaded handgun he had found in his parents' bedroom when it discharged, killing him. According to the paediatrician Vincent Ianelli, there were 122 unintentional firearm deaths of children in America in 2007, and an additional 3,060 non-fatal shooting accidents, and the numbers have remained about the same since. Most of these children would have been repeatedly warned, at school and at home, that guns are dangerous, but still could not resist picking them up. Self-preservation is our most deep-rooted instinct. But curiosity is powerful enough to override it.

The day they picked up the gun, Brian and his brother had been seized by 'diversive curiosity' – the desire for novelty. Children vibrate with diversive curiosity; it powers their unceasing explorations. It's the desire to see what happens when I put my hand in this flame, or dirt in my mouth, or a gun in my hand. In our adult lives it generates a restless desire for new information and new experiences. Just as it made us peer into rock pools as children, as adults it makes us refresh Twitter streams.[*]

Diversive curiosity follows no particular process or method, but slides from one novel object of attention to the next. Boredom is furiously averted or deferred, new information and sensations are constantly sought out. It is impulsive and irresistible; it *seizes* us. In a variation on the famous marshmallow test, in which a child is presented with a treat and asked if he can resist eating it for five minutes, experimenters ask children not to turn around to look at an attractive toy behind them, and observe whether they can resist the temptation to do so. Few can.

It's not just children. St Augustine told the story of Alypius from Rome, who detested and was utterly opposed to gladiatorial shows. On the day of one of these shows, he bumped into some friends who virtually dragged him along to the amphitheatre. Stubbornly, Alypius closed his eyes as

---

[*] Perceptual curiosity, which diversive curiosity encompasses, refers specifically to the seeking out of physical experience – it is what drives people up mountains and down rivers, just to see what's there.

the show began. But when the crowd roared he was 'overcome by curiosity' and took a peek. He was, recounts St Augustine, scarred for life.

Diversive curiosity can be a strength, leading people to take in more from their environment. But it can quickly become aimless, distracting and frustrating. In a 1993 study, researchers interviewed thirty people about their mail delivery, and found that while people looked forward to their daily post with anticipation and impatience, most reported almost always being disappointed by the actual mail they received. In the era of email and social media, this compulsive cycle of anticipation and disappointment is repeated dozens if not hundreds of times a day.

Though he calls it simply 'curiosity', the eighteenth-century thinker Edmund Burke captures the nature of diversive curiosity perfectly:

The first and the simplest emotion which we discover in the human mind, is Curiosity. By curiosity, I mean whatever desire we have for, or whatever pleasure we take in, novelty. We see children perpetually running from place to place, to hunt out something new: they catch with great eagerness, and with very little choice, at whatever comes before them; their attention is engaged by everything, because everything has, in that stage of life, the charm of novelty to recommend it. But as those things which engage us merely by their novelty, cannot attach us for any length of time, curiosity is the most superficial of all the affections; it changes its object perpetu-

ally, it has an appetite which is very sharp, but very easily
satisfied; and it has always an appearance of giddiness, rest-
lessness, and anxiety.

It's odd to hear Burke rail against curiosity like this because
he himself was what we might think of as a deeply curious
man, interested in everything from the meaning of beauty
to the living conditions of Britain's colonial subjects. But
as we shall see, curiosity's connection to learning took hold
relatively recently – in fact, it started around the time that
Burke was writing.

Diversive curiosity is where the hunt for knowledge
begins; in the desire for new information, sensations, experiences and challenges. But it's only a beginning. If there's
something oddly familiar about Burke's description, that's
probably because it might be used to describe the way we
often use the web: clicking from link to link, searching for
the new thing without ever stopping long enough to learn
or absorb what's in front of us. In our digital world, diversive
curiosity is constantly stimulated by ever-present streams of
texts, emails, tweets, reminders and news alerts that stimulate our hunger for novelty. In the process, our capacity
for the slow, difficult and frustrating process of gathering
knowledge may be deteriorating.

When he was thirty-eight Alexander Arguelles concluded,
regretfully, that he knew too many languages. It was 2001
and he had just returned to South Korea after a month's

stay in St Petersburg, where he had taken one-on-one lessons in Russian with a private tutor for six hours a day. By the time he left St Petersburg he felt able to hold his own with natives of the Russian tongue. But when he got back to his small house in the Korean countryside and sat down to read Turgenev and Dostoyevsky in the original, he found himself in over his head. His grasp of the Russian vocabulary was insufficient to appreciate the greatest works of that language. A painful choice confronted him.

Ever since he was a boy, Arguelles has been endlessly hungry for languages to learn. Born and raised in New York, as a child he travelled widely with his family across India, North Africa and Europe, staying for a while in Italy. His father was a self-taught polyglot, and Arguelles grew up observing him switch effortlessly from language to language depending on who he was talking to. His father, whom he remembers as an intimidating figure, didn't encourage him to take his lead. But Alexander had been bitten by the linguistic bug.

Learning languages certainly didn't come naturally to him. He made slow progress with French at school and nearly gave it up. But he persisted, and eventually found that he enjoyed the challenge of new languages. When he was fourteen he started reading German writers and philosophers in translation, like Goethe and Immanuel Kant. He knew he would have to learn German to a high standard if he was to read them in their native tongue, and so really understand, at the deepest level, their ideas. At university, more languages gave up their mysteries to him: French, Latin, Ancient Greek and Sanskrit. Arguelles became fascinated by the idea of having an *encyclopaedic* mind – one that gave him a panoptic view of the world's accumulated wisdom. He set his heart on learning as many languages as he could.

After graduating, he went on to study the history of religion at the University of Chicago, where he signed up for classes in Persian and Old French, though they weren't relevant to his doctorate. One day, Arguelles was summoned to the office of his advisor, who asked him why he was attending Persian classes instead of devoting his time to the study of religion. Arguelles answered candidly: he just loved learning languages. His advisor shook his head. You will not be taken seriously as a scholar, he said, with that attitude. You have to choose.

Arguelles was forced to drop Persian but got away with continuing to study Old French, Old German, Old English and Norse. After Chicago he moved to Berlin where he held a post-doctoral fellowship in German philology. His passion for language again held sway, consuming more energy that his official course of study. Arguelles was determined to become as fluent in German as a native speaker. He abolished English from his speech and even from his thoughts. He asked acquaintances to correct every mistake that he made, looked up every new expression he encountered, and met a professional phonetician every week to perfect his accent. After a while, he stopped worrying about how to speak German and simply began to live in it.

His fellowship enabled him to travel widely across Europe, and he used the opportunity to learn yet more languages. He discovered that languages which seemed quite different on the surface shared hidden similarities; each new language became like a variation on a theme rather than a new entity to be learned from scratch. The languages in his head began speaking to each other. Swedish revealed itself to be a combination of languages he already knew: Norse, Old German and English. After three weeks of study, he was able to hold his own in complex conversations with native Swedes.

Not that it ever became easy. 'There is no secret,' he says, except 'hours of concentration.' Arguelles didn't only have to study hard to learn more languages; he had to develop a new personality. A naturally reticent man, he forced himself to become garrulous, seeking out conversations he would otherwise have avoided, with natives of whichever language he was learning.

Arguelles still craved 'a real linguistic challenge'. He decided to attempt mastery of Asian languages, and took up a post at a university in South Korea (he had read that Korean was considered to be the most challenging of all Asian languages for a Westerner to learn). The campus was on an isolated hill amidst pine and bamboo forests and rice fields, and Arguelles' room had a view of the Pacific Ocean. For the next five years he settled into an almost monastic routine, going to sleep at 8 p.m. and rising at 2 a.m., studying for sixteen hours each day. He learned Korean, Mandarin, Japanese and Malay-Indonesian. He explored the Celtic and

Slavic families, made forays into Finnish, Zulu, Swahili, Ancient Egyptian and Quechua, and became at home in Arabic and Persian.

It was only after his trip to Russia that Arguelles realised that he would have to abandon many of the languages he had begun to learn, in order to go deeper into the ones he already knew.

The stories of Brian Smith and Alexander Arguelles appear to have little in common. But they are both examples, albeit unusual ones, of the same thing: the deepening of a simple urge to explore into an enduring desire to learn.

There are two sides of curiosity. One compels us to turn over stones, open cupboards and click on links; the kind that can make the high-minded professor prise open the pages of the glossy magazine in front of her and the teenager slip a cigarette out of his mother's pack. The other makes us want to spend time finishing long novels and pursuing interests that have nothing to do with our self-interest, like learning dead languages. What distinguishes one from the other is the accumulation of specialised knowledge.

Brian Smith never mentioned what happened with the gun that night to any of his siblings. He escaped any repercussions, including what he knew would have been a fearsome punishment from his mother. But the incident left its mark on him in another way. He turned his dangerous curiosity about guns into an enduring desire to learn about them, and became educated about them in a way that went far beyond the cursory explanation of their dangers offered to most kids at school.* As an adult, Smith became a police officer in Chicago, and gained special expertise in the use of firearms. Over the years he trained thousands of law enforcement officers in their operation, including a team deployed to protect Hillary Clinton when she was first lady. Now he is retired from the force, Smith looks back on that evening and reflects on the dangers of 'untutored curiosity'.

Alexander Arguelles started out wanting to learn languages because being multilingual seemed like an exciting prospect. He soon found that the more he learned, the more he could explore. As he grew older, his curiosity deepened into a desire to absorb the wisdom of the world's finest minds.† Without a knowledge of guns, Brian Smith's desire to explore them was dangerous; but then again, without a desire to explore he might not have accumulated the expertise that he did. Epistemic curiosity represents the deepening of a simple seeking of newness into a *directed* attempt to build understanding. It's what happens when diversive curiosity grows up.

Epistemic curiosity is hard work; it involves sustained

---

* Of course, one obvious way to reduce the danger of firearms is to restrict their availability, but that debate is beyond the scope of this book: I use guns here simply as an extreme example of the power of diversive curiosity.

† Just as he was coming to terms with his decision to unlearn some languages, Arguelles' life changed; he met the woman he was to marry, a Korean, and became a father. He now lives with his family in California, where he continues his studies.

cognitive *effort*. That makes it tougher, but ultimately more rewarding. Just as the resistance offered by a tungsten filament to electrons generates light in a light bulb, it's the very difficulty of exercising epistemic curiosity that brings illumination.

In its raw, impulsive form, curiosity deserves its reputation for danger, as Brian Smith will attest. The explorations that toddlers make can lead them into trouble – that's why adults put gates at the top of the stairs. High diversive curiosity is counted as a risk factor for drug addiction and arson; experts say that one the reasons children start fires is that they are overwhelmed by curiosity to see what something looks like when it is set alight.

'There's absolutely no financial gain to knowing languages,' Arguelles told an interviewer recently. 'It's a waste of time and energy.' Why do we take risks to achieve knowledge that has no immediate use or benefit? Economists find this hard to explain, because it doesn't fit their models of human behaviour. It's also hard to understand from an evolutionary standpoint. If our primary goal is to survive long enough to pass on our genes, why are we born with this apparent need to put our well-being at risk, or at least to create difficulty and uncertainty where before there was none? To put it another way, why is *Homo sapiens* such a curious animal?

Imagine a human hunter, armed only with a rudimentary stone weapon like a slingshot, looking for an animal to kill and eat. First, he has to find it, and then he has to get relatively close to it, because his weapon has a short range. Then he has to kill it before getting killed himself. It is a complex problem. Solving it requires knowledge.

The hunter has to know how to read animal tracks, so that he can work out which animal has left them, in which direction it is moving, and – judging by their freshness – how far away it might be. He may also be able to glean clues as to the age of the animal, its sex, size and physical condition. Then, when he is closing in on it, he has to deploy his knowledge of animal behaviour to predict its next move – for instance, whether snorting or salivating indicates that it is about to attack, or take flight, and in either case, how fast the animal is likely to move.* It's unlikely that this will be a solo mission – he'll probably be hunting in a group. But that only makes things more complex; now he has to know what the roles of each member of the group is, what their strengths and weaknesses are, and who he can and cannot trust.

---

* In 1973 the evolutionary psychologists Steven Tulkin and Melvin Konner spent time with Kalahari Bushmen, and discovered that they not only had a remarkable amount of knowledge about animal behaviour, but sophisticated methods of evaluating it. The distinctions the Kalahari made included: *1. I saw it with my own eyes; 2. I didn't see it with my eyes but I saw the tracks. Here is how I inferred it from the tracks; 3. I didn't see it with my own eyes or see the tracks but I heard it from many people who saw it (or a few, or one); 4. It's not certain because I didn't see it with my own eyes or talk directly with people who saw it.*

37

Knowing stuff was always important to the survival of humans and their forebears, particularly because they were physically weaker than some of their adversaries, and at some point in their evolution humans evolved capacious memories, which meant they could afford to make *speculative investments* in knowledge. Rather than simply seeking out the information they needed at the time they needed it – when they were hungry, for instance – they could gather and store information for use at a later date. One exploratory expedition could yield information that might be used many times over during their lifetime – or never at all.

Stephen Kaplan, an evolutionary psychologist at the University of Michigan, describes the early human as 'a far-ranging and yet home-based animal'. The more information about her environment a human acquired, the more likely she would be to survive and pass on her genes. Gathering that knowledge meant venturing out into the unknown, to spot new sources of water or edible plants. But doing so meant risking one's survival; you might become vulnerable to predators, or get lost. The individuals more likely to survive would have been those adept at striking a balance between knowledge-gathering and self-preservation.

Perhaps as an incentive to take a few risks in the pursuit of new information, evolution tied the act of curiosity to pleasure. Most of us know what Copernicus meant when he described the 'unbelievable pleasure of the spirit' he found in learning. Neuroscientists have located this pleasure in one of the brain's chemical messengers. Scientists at the

California Institute of Technology asked undergraduates forty trivia questions while in a brain scanner. After reading each question, the subjects were told to silently guess the answer, and to indicate their curiosity about the correct answer. Then, they saw the question presented again, followed by the answer. The questions which stoked their curiosity were stimulating their caudate nucleus, a part of the brain associated with both learning and romantic love. The caudate nucleus is closely packed with neurons which traffic in dopamine, a chemical that surges through our brains when we enjoy sex or food. As the brain has evolved, it seems to have bootstrapped the urge for intellectual investigation onto the same pathway as our most primal pleasures.*

The caudate nucleus has also been implicated in our responses to visual beauty, and there may be a deep connection between our aesthetic predilections and our hunger for knowledge. Numerous studies have shown that when people from different cultures are presented with pictures of landscapes, they prefer those that show scenes from nature, and in particular, those that feature water sources — rivers, oceans, waterfalls. That suggests we are unconsciously assessing how we might get along were we dropped into the environment we're looking at.

But what's really interesting is that the most consistent

---

* The feeling of being interested can act as a kind of neurological signal, directing us to fruitful areas of enquiry. B.F. Skinner, the great experimental psychologist, advised, 'When you run into something interesting, drop everything else and study it.'

and universal predictor of preference in these studies is *mystery*, scenes that hint at something the viewer cannot see – a winding path leading off into the distance, or dense foliage with a hint of a gap through which one could pass. The reassuring presence of something we know is good for us gives us pleasure. But so does the promise of what lies beyond, the information we don't yet know.[*]

About 60,000 years ago a small population of humans journeyed out of Africa and struck out for the unknown. They left their primate cousins behind, along with the ecological niche they had shared with them. Nearly all animals are confined to their niches: gorillas do not seek to leave the jungle and make a home in the river; mackerel aren't foolhardy enough to see if they can make it on the land; tree frogs stick close to trees. But when humans left the savannah, they took up residency on coasts, in deserts and forests, on mountains, plains and ice caps; even in outer space. In all these places, they built specially designed

---

[*] Stephen Kaplan connects this work to an influential theory of landscape preference proposed by Jay Appleton, a British geographer, in his 1975 book, *The Experience of Landscape*. Drawing on examples from art and from the real world, Appleton argued that people look for two things in a landscape: *prospect* and *refuge*. Prospect refers to the enjoyment we get from an overview of the scene. Refuge is the suggestion of safe places to hide, where one can see without being seen. You can think about this in terms of information preference – we like to gather information, and we enjoy having information advantages over others (sometimes we call them 'secrets').

shelters and invented new ways of getting around. They made themselves at home.

What makes us so adaptable? In one word, culture – our ability learn from others, to copy, imitate, share and improve. When humans learned to communicate using oral and, later, written language, ideas, knowledge and practices – how to carve a fishhook, build a boat, make a spear, sing a song or carve a god – could replicate and combine like genes. But unlike genes, they could jump from one mind to another across distances of time and space. Culture freed humans from the limitations of their biology; according to the evolutionary biologist Mark Pagel, when humans discovered culture they achieved a momentous shift in the balance of power 'between our genes and our minds'. Humans became the only species to acquire guidance on how to live from the accumulated knowledge of their ancestors, rather than just from their DNA.

Humans can learn from peers – 'horizontal learning' – and from parents and elders – 'vertical learning'. We can also learn from our ancestors. This ability to pass on knowledge, not just to each other, but down generations, is what makes us so adaptive, inventive and imaginative. Knowledge builds on knowledge, ideas on ideas. That we no longer have to invent the wheel enables us to invent the automobile. As Pagel puts it, 'Having culture is why we watch 3D TV and build cathedrals while our close genetic relatives, chimps, sit in the forest as they have for millions of years cracking the same nuts and stones.'

A cultural animal must be a curious animal. Evolution

has selected for the ability to absorb culture as surely as it selected for our instinct to run away from angry bears. As the developmental psychologist Alison Gopnik says, 'For human beings, nurture *is* our nature.' Epistemic curiosity — a desire for cultural information — was one of the traits that enabled humans not just to journey out of Africa but to put down roots in every corner of the world. Diversive curiosity makes us want to know what lies on the other side of the mountain; epistemic curiosity arms us with the knowledge we need to survive when we get there. Every human society is, in Mark Pagel's words, a 'cultural survival vehicle', rich in accumulated knowledge. Every baby is born with a powerful urge to explore it.

Once they have acquired what they need to know in order to get by, some adults cease striving to learn from those around them. Others continue to explore with the ardour of a child. On a page from Leonardo da Vinci's notebooks is a to-do list. Here is an edited version, in translation:

- *Calculate the measurement of Milan and its suburbs.*
- *Find a book that treats of Milan its churches, which is to be had at the stationer's on the way to Cordusio.*
- *Discover the measurement of the Corte Vecchio [courtyard of the Duke's palace]*
- *Get the Master of Arithmetic to show you how to square a triangle.*
- *Ask Benedetto Portinari [a Florentine merchant] by what means they go on ice at Flanders?*

- *Draw Milan.*
- *Ask Maestro Antonio how mortars are positioned on bastions by day or night.*
- *Examine the crossbow of Maestro Gianetto.*
- *Find a Master of Hydraulics and get him to tell you how to repair a lock, canal and mill, in the Lombard manner.*
- *Ask about the measurement of the sun, promised me by Maestro Giovanni Francese.*

Perhaps the first thing that you notice about this list is the dazzling diversity of Leonardo's interests. He is eager to learn about everything, from the distance of the sun from the earth, to the workings of a crossbow, to ice skating in Flanders (and in between investigating them he will 'draw Milan' – and, perhaps, paint the *Mona Lisa*).

Life would be more straightforward if we knew what we need to find out; if we were told at birth, exactly what we need to know to be happy. But in a complex world, it's impossible to know what might be useful in the future. It's important, therefore, to spread your cognitive bets. Curious people take risks, try things out, allow themselves to get productively distracted. They know that something they learn by chance today may well come in useful tomorrow, or spark a new way of thinking about an entirely different problem. The more unpredictable the environment, the more important a seemingly unnecessary breadth and depth of knowledge becomes. Humans have always had to deal with complexity; felling a woolly mammoth is not simple. But now that we live in larger, more varied, faster-changing societies than ever before, curiosity is more important – and more rewarding – than it has ever been.

This applies to *who* we need to know, as well as what. Another striking thing about Leonardo's list is how many house visits he will have to make. His curiosity makes him highly sociable. Montaigne wrote of how travel to different regions and countries allows us to 'rub and polish our brains' against others, and Leonardo seems keen to polish his brain against as many others as possible. Out of the fifteen tasks in the complete list, at least eight involve consultations with other people, and two involve other people's books. It is easy to imagine Leonardo eagerly approaching each expert, intent on drawing out their knowledge, beginning each conversation with '*Dimmi* . . .'. People who are deeply curious are more likely to be good at collaboration. They seek out new acquaintances and allies in the process of building their stock of cultural knowledge.

In the next chapter we'll look more closely at the curiosity of babies and children, and at why some of them are more likely than others to grow into adults who share Leonardo's passionate curiosity.

CHAPTER 2

How Curiosity Begins

If you were deciding which of the world's neighbourhoods scores highest for epistemic curiosity, Bloomsbury in London would be a strong candidate. At its heart is the British Museum, a global hub of enquiry and intellectual exchange for over 250 years. Stroll down streets lined with elegant Georgian townhouses and mansion blocks, and your eye is caught by blue plaques denoting the former residences and workplaces of some of the modern world's most influential thinkers: Charles Darwin, Bertrand Russell, Virginia Woolf, John Maynard Keynes. Today those streets are thronged by the students and faculty of the University of London and its associated institutions.

Push through the door of an anonymous-looking building just off Russell Square, and you find yourself at the entrance to a brightly coloured playroom full of toys. It's not a crèche, but the reception area for Babylab, where the mysteries of infant minds are studied. Babylab was created as part of Birkbeck College's drive to become a globally renowned centre for the study of early cognitive development. Every week, dozens of tiny research subjects arrive, accompanied by their parent or carer, to play games in the name of science, enabling Birkbeck's researchers to get a little closer to understanding what's going on inside the newly minted human brain.

On a February afternoon at Babylab I meet two psychologists who are investigating the origins of epistemic curiosity: Teodora Gliga and Katarina Begus (Begus is studying for her PhD, Gliga is her supervisor). Gliga and Begus introduce me to their new research subject. Guiu, whose mother is from Barcelona, is nine months old. He is given a toy phone to play with while Katarina deftly slips a net of electrodes over his head. He is then carried into a small room with a camera in it, where, with the help of his mother, Katarina straps him into a chair facing a TV screen.

For the next five minutes a succession of toys of varying shapes and sizes are handed to Guiu by Katarina, while his mother stands by. Just outside the room, Teodora and I can view Guiu's reactions to the toys on two screens. One is a video feed, which will later be studied to assess how interested Guiu was in what was in front of him – how long he played with each toy, and where his gaze were directed. The other screen shows a series of wobbly parallel lines that spike unpredictably; this shows us roughly what's going on in Guiu's brain, as measured by the electrical activity detected by his electrode hairnet.

It's easy to imagine that infants are in a permanent state

of curiosity. Books on parenting, popular science accounts, and our incorrigibly sentimental view of children all conspire to suggest that babies spend every waking second lost in wonder. But although they are avidly inquisitive creatures, the curiosity of babies wanes and waxes, just as ours does. Sometimes babies are primed and ready to learn; other times they are bored, or lost to imaginings, or just sleepy. Crucially, their level of curiosity is acutely responsive to what's around them – to their physical environment, and, above all, to their adult carers. Infant curiosity is co-dependent.

Gliga and Begus are trying to find a reliable way of measuring the extent of a baby's curiosity at any one moment. They have been running experiments, like the one I am witnessing today, to see if they can identify the particular state of the infant brain in the moment of epistemic curiosity. Their hypothesis, which they are still exploring (working with babies, like parenting, requires immense patience), is that there is a particular neurological state, identifiable via a particular brain wave, which represents the moment when a baby is most willing and able to acquire knowledge.

Once Guiu has been presented with all the toys in Katarina's box, his attention is captured by some colourful imagery on the TV screen in front of him. A series of images of the toys that he was just playing with is played back. Next to each is an image of a toy that bears a strong resemblance to it but is subtly different. When Gliga and Begus study the data from this experiment they will look to see if there is any correlation between the amount of time and energy Guiu spends looking at the slightly different version of a particular toy and the amount of interest he previously showed in the original toy. Their reasoning is that if Guiu looks harder at the similar-but-different image of a toy it's because he was interested in the original toy and is now *eager to learn more about it.*

His curiosity has been piqued.

Imagine a group of parents from different species getting together for a coffee and discussing the progress of their offspring. The foal's father would be boasting that his son virtually walked out of the womb; the sheep's mother would be complaining about her young daughter's choice of sexual partner. Everyone would feel sorry for the human parents. *Three years old, and barely able to feed itself.*

As a species, we are embarrassingly slow to mature. Foals are tottering around the paddock within half an hour of leaving the maternal womb; babies aren't toddling until they are about eighteen months old. Birds are evicted from the nest by their mothers within a couple of months; humans move back into the parental home after college. Chimps go straight from weaning to puberty, while humans take another decade or so. Alison Gopnik points out that, 'No creature spends more time dependent on others for its very existence than a human baby, and no creature takes on the burden of that dependence so long and so readily as a human adult.' We call this protracted period of dependence on adults 'childhood'.

How Curiosity Begins

Our extended infancy has a hidden upside – it bequeaths the mature human a child's capacity to love, learn and wonder why. Childhood means not having to commit to particular courses of action, because adults are taking care of our survival. We can hang back, watch, question, and learn what works best for us before deciding which paths to take. Ultimately it's this that make *Homo sapiens* so adaptable and inventive (no wonder we find the fable of the tortoise and the hare so appealing). Without the necessity to fend for ourselves in those first ten or twenty years, we can focus on learning about the niche into which we have been born, and form our own ideas about it.

That involves getting to know our physical environment, whether that be an igloo on the ice or a house in Islington. It also means learning to navigate our *cultural* environment – the world of gesture, symbol, and technology in which we find ourselves. John Locke, the seventeenth-century English philosopher, famously conceived of the infant mind as a *tabula rasa* or blank slate. We now know that this is not literally true; scientists believe that babies are born with certain fundamental abilities: to imitate, to recognise faces, to discern basic causal relationships. But Locke's insight, born from his revulsion at the violent intolerance that had seen England degenerate into a civil war between Catholics and Protestants, endures.

Nobody is born Catholic or Protestant, Eskimo or Bedouin. Your sense of identity, of being a person, is formed by the cultural knowledge you learn, first from your parents and then from others. If culture is the citadel that keeps us safe and allows us to thrive (or sets us against one another), babies use curiosity like a rope to pull themselves over its battlements – and adults throw the rope down to them.

Children are agents of their own learning. Rather than simply taking in information from their environment or following genetic instructions, babies make it their own business to find out about the world. Put a baby down anywhere and it will start stroking, licking, picking things up and putting them in its mouth, and later, crawling, walking and running.

Scientists at the National Institute of Child Health and Human Development in Maryland recently discovered something extraordinary – the more actively a baby explores his or her environment, the more likely it is that he or she will go on to achieve academic success as an adolescent. The researchers measured the propensity of 374 five-month-old babies to crawl and probe and fiddle, and then tracked their progress over the following fourteen years. They found that the ones doing best at school aged fourteen were the ones who had been the most energetically exploratory babies.

But it is in the social world, and the cultures in which our social worlds exist, that babies and toddlers really exert and build their cognitive muscles. Any parent of a young child will know that small children love to run psychological tests on adults, testing their limits. The naughtiness of infants is experimental, a method of data collection. When a mother tells her son not to eat dirt he immediately wonders what will happen if he does, and how his mother will react. The child who pushes over his elder sister's carefully constructed tower of play blocks is doing so not just to watch the structure collapse, but to see his sister explode.

At first, children hypothesise that there is no difference between what others are thinking and what they are thinking; that everyone is thinking the same thing. Then they notice that the theory doesn't hold – different people seem to say and want different things, becoming upset when they don't get them or happy when they do. That's when children become interested in what's going on in those other minds – when empathic curiosity begins. Before even this stage, children are sophisticated mimics, imitating adult behaviour even when they don't know why they're doing so, yet quite capable of discriminating between the adults worth imitating and those best ignored.

All this time, they are gathering cultural information – learning how to express themselves, about right and wrong, about what's considered acceptable behaviour and unacceptable behaviour. One of the most important things they learn about is whether it's good to learn.

Right from the beginning, curiosity is a joint venture.

Begus and Gliga are seeking to unlock one of the mysteries of child development – why some babies grow into highly curious children, and others don't. Their working hypothesis is that there are two factors involved: first, the child's basic cognitive ability, or intelligence, and second, the responses children receive to their nascent enquiries from parents and carers in those first years.

One of Begus and Gliga's experiments centres on a deceptively simple action – pointing. Most babies start to gesture towards things sometime around their first birthday, and soon they are doing so with their index finger. When a child points, she is initiating what psychologists call 'joint attention' – getting you to pay attention to what she's paying attention to. Pointing is crucial to childhood development; the frequency with which a child points correlates to the speed with which she acquires language. Children who don't point tend to have difficulties in learning language, following social cues and learning from others.

It's impossible to know for sure *why* babies point, because they can't tell us. But we can make good guesses; for instance, that they are pointing to things they want, or simply to engage their mother's attention. Gliga and Begus think that infants often point to something to signal their *interest* in it. The child wants to know more about something, and expects their parent to tell them about it. Before they are able to speak, they are asking a question with their finger.

In one study, conducted with sixteen-month-old babies, Begus played games with the babies which involved everyday objects with which the infants were familiar, like a book or a cup, together with some unfamiliar toys that Begus had made herself. She and the baby explored the objects together. With some babies, Begus acted as you would expect a knowledgeable adult to – she named the familiar objects correctly and helped the baby label and explore the unfamiliar objects when the baby pointed at them. With other babies, Begus played the fool – she pretended not to know what the familiar objects were, or got them all wrong, calling a cup a shoe. What she found was that the babies in the second condition were much less likely to engage in pointing behaviour than the babies in the first condition.

It is sobering to think that even at an early age, infants are quite capable of telling whether or not you're an idiot – a judgement which, when you think about it, demands substantial cognitive and social abilities. But this had been shown before. What was new about this study was its evidence that pointing is about learning from others, and that whether or not children point depends on the adult they're with. When faced with someone clearly ignorant or unreliable, babies stop pointing. If you're unlikely to give them good information, there's no point.

The same principles apply to a baby's babbling. Babies start to babble a few months after birth, and they do so in similar ways all over the world, regardless of which culture they are from. After writing this behaviour off as unimportant for many years, scientists now think of it as a key marker of cognitive and social development, and an essential precursor to speech. Michael Goldstein, an associate professor of psychology at Cornell University, has looked at how babies learn the names of objects they are unfamiliar with. He found that they are more likely to learn these new words when they are offered in response to the baby's babbling. 'In that moment of babbling, babies seem to be primed to take in more information,' he says. 'It's about creating a social interaction where now you can learn new things.'

Babbling, like pointing, is a sign of readiness to learn, and babies are also more likely to use it as a tool of their curiosity if their parents respond to it as such; if, rather than ignoring them, they try and answer whatever they think the baby's unintelligible question might be. If a baby looks at an apple and says 'Da da da!' and the adult says nothing, the baby not only fails to learn the name of that round greenish object, she also starts to think that this whole babbling business might be a waste of time.

Curiosity supercharges learning, even in these early months and years. In a separate study, Begus showed two novel objects to each baby. The toys were like simple puzzles, responding in interesting ways to pushes or pulls or brushes in the right places. After presenting the two objects, Begus waited for the baby to point to one of them. Then she demonstrated how one of the objects worked, choosing either the object the baby pointed to, or the one he hadn't. Next, Begus took the objects away and, ten minutes later, brought them back to observe whether or not the baby played with them in the way they had been shown. Babies were much more likely to replicate her actions correctly with the object in which they had been interested in the first place.

It's remarkable that even in the course of fifteen minutes in the laboratory, an adult can elicit a lot or a little curiosity from an infant, depending on how she behaves. But this is one of the secrets of curiosity. We don't get allocated a fixed amount of it at birth. Instead, we inherit a mercurial quality that rises and falls through the day, and throughout our lives. What's more, its progress is deeply affected by the behaviour of people around us, especially in those first months and years.

In the same study, Begus observed the infants at play with their parents. She found that children whose parents responded more to their promptings, and asked more questions in return, were the children who learned most about how their chosen object could be used. Here, then, is the most likely answer to the question that Begus and Gliga are investigating – to a surprisingly large extent, whether or not a child is highly curious or incurious depends how their parents responded to these early unspoken queries. Curiosity is a feedback loop.

What do children think pointing is for? That depends on how they see adults react when they do it. 'If they just get *given* the object they're pointing to, they learn that the function of pointing is getting things,' Gliga told me. 'If they get *told the name* of the object, then they learn to think of it as a way of getting information.' What happens if they get neither, I asked – if they receive no response to their signal?

'They stop pointing.'

*

In most ways, children become more independent of adults as they grow older. But when it comes to curiosity, adults become *more* important to children as time goes by.

As any parent knows, children ask questions – a lot of questions. In 2007 the psychologist Michelle Chouinard analysed recordings of four children interacting with their respective caregivers for two hours at a time, for a total of over 200 hours. She found that, on average, the children posed over a hundred questions *every hour*. Some of the questions were requests or calls for attention, but about two thirds were designed to elicit information, e.g., 'What is the name for that?' Question-asking, concluded Chouinard, 'is not something that happens every now and then – asking questions is a central part of what it means to be a child.'

As children grow older, their questions become more probing; they start to ask for explanations, rather than just information. Chouinard found that up until the age of about thirty months, children mostly ask *what* and *where* questions: 'What's that?', 'What does it do?', 'Where is my ball?' or (of a sibling or a pet) 'What is he doing?' These are questions designed to elicit facts. Then, sometime around their third birthday, they start to ask *how* and *why* questions; questions designed to elicit *explanation*.* This type of question becomes more frequent as the child grows. When conversing

---

* *How* or *why* questions may not literally include the words 'how' or 'why'. Paul Harris uses the example of a child looking at a broken toy airplane and asking 'Daddy broke?' As Harris says, 'the child is probably seeking explanatory information, even if the question is not well formed.'

with a familiar adult at home, preschoolers ask explanatory questions at a rate of about twenty-five times an hour.

Paul Harris, a professor of education at Harvard, is an expert on children's question-asking. Extrapolating from Chouinard's data, he estimates that between the ages of two and five, children ask a total of 40,000 'explanatory' questions. 'That's an amazing number,' he says. 'It shows that questioning is an incredibly important engine for cognitive development.' These explanatory questions can be profound or silly, perceptive or incomprehensible, stirring or hilarious. Here's a random sample of questions from my friends' children, all of whom were under ten years old when they asked them:

- *When I am sixteen will all of you adults be dead?*
- *What happens if your eyes turn into flies?*
- *What is time?*
- *Did you used to be a monkey?*
- *Why can't I run away from my shadow?*
- *If I'm made from a bit of mummy and a bit of daddy then where does the bit that's me come from?*
- *Will I die on the cross like Jesus?*

Paul Harris points out that asking a question requires a complex mental process. 'The child has to first realise that there are things they *don't know* . . . that there are invisible worlds of knowledge they have never visited.' They also have to realise that other people are information-bearing agents, and that language can be used as 'a tool for shifting stuff from that person to them'. The question is a technology that children use to trawl for insights. As Harris remarks, it's striking that the questions children ask aren't restricted to immediate goals, like what's for dinner or how to make a toy work. 'They probe the how and why of things, sometimes tenaciously, even if it yields no tangible rewards.' Every question is a little bet. From a very young age, children sense that any information they can gather, even it doesn't have an immediate application, may come in useful in the future. Some of their questions will lead to dead ends, confusions or refusals from embarrassed parents. But, cumulatively, their questions bring knowledge, and with more knowledge, the child knows that he is growing, just as surely as he knows he will exceed this year's chalk mark on the wall chart next year.

The incuriosity of Kanzi – the highly intelligent bonobo ape – wasn't a mere problem of linguistic complexity. Michelle Chouinard noted that even before they learn language, children can vocalise information-gathering questions. For example, one mother was unpacking her groceries when her child picked up an unfamiliar item – a kiwi fruit – and held it towards her mother with a puzzled expression on her face and the monosyllabic but perfectly expressive question, 'Uh?' Children sometimes ask questions simply by repeating what they have just heard. Researchers observed two three-year-old twins, David and Toby, talking to each other. David said, 'My hands are cold.' 'Cold?' asked Toby.

Kanzi doesn't even do this. Unlike human children, Kanzi doesn't seem to have grasped that communication can be an exchange of information, or that there are others who know more about the world than he does. Children intuitively understand, says Harris, that adults can be 'trustworthy informers about hidden reality'. Children are scientists, experimenting on their physical environment, but they are also investigative reporters, pumping their sources for secrets.

We're so used to the idea of being able to ask questions that we've forgotten what an amazing skill, or set of skills, it is. First, you have to know that you don't know – to conceive of your own ignorance. Second, you have to be able to imagine different, competing possibilities; when a child asks whether ghosts are real or made-up, she is already imagining alternative explanations. Third, you have to understand that you can learn from other people. None of these abilities are shared by other primates, and neither is their development in human children simple or inevitable; under different conditions, they can flourish or atrophy.

When we're adults, we can shape those conditions in the right way, as long as we know how to do so. But a young child can't do this. Her curiosity is shaped for her, by parents and carers. Most parents, including this one, can get impatient with the incessant curiosity of children – with their pointing, babbling and question-asking. It's hard to engage with every one of our child's enquiries when we're trying to make dinner, talk to a friend, finish an email or just relax.

CURIOUS

These days it's increasingly easy to fob them off to our electronic child-minders. Technology is a great aid in getting parents off the hook of their children's curiosity; we can drop them in front of the TV, give them a cellphone to play with, or hand them an iPad with their favourite game on it. It's not the worst thing you can do to a child. But after talking to the experts and learning about how children learn, I'm now painfully aware that every time I ignore my daughter's questions, I may be stunting her innate desire to know.

CHAPTER 3

Puzzles and Mysteries

Henry James remarked, wistfully, that 'our purely intellectual zeal' ebbs as we become adults. 'In each of us a saturation-point is soon reached . . . we settle into an equilibrium and live on what we learned when our interest was fresh and instinctive'. According to the educational psychologist Susan Engel, curiosity begins to wane as young as four years old. By the time we are adults we have fewer questions, and more default settings. As James put it, 'Disinterested curiosity is past, the mental grooves and channels set.'

The decline in curiosity can be traced in the development of the brain through childhood. Though smaller than the adult brain, the infant brain contains millions more neural connections. The wiring, however, is a mess; the lines of communication between infant neurons are far less efficient than between those in the adult brain. The baby's perception of the world is consequently both intensely rich and wildly disordered. As children absorb more evidence from the world around them, certain possibilities become much more likely and more useful, and harden into knowledge, or beliefs. The neural pathways that enable those beliefs become faster and more automatic, while the ones that the child doesn't use regularly are pruned away. An overgrown garden becomes less abundant and more orderly.*

This waning of curiosity is not necessarily a bad thing. It's essential in becoming a person who can act on the world, rather than one helplessly in thrall to it, hostage to every passing stimulus. Computer scientists talk about the difference between *exploring* and *exploiting* – a system will learn more if it explores many possibilities, but it will be more effective if it simply acts on the most likely one. As babies grow into children and then into adults, they begin to do more exploiting of whatever knowledge they have acquired. As adults, however, we have a tendency to err too far towards exploitation – we become content to fall back on the stock of knowledge and mental habits we built up when we were young, rather than adding to or revising it. We get lazy.

In finding the right balance between these two strategies, it's helpful to understand how curiosity works. This isn't a simple question. Over the years, psychologists have had a hard time getting to grips with curiosity despite, presumably, being on intimate terms with it themselves.

---

* This process continues right into early adulthood – the prefrontal cortex, a part of the brain behind the forehead which controls and directs our attention, doesn't fully take shape until our early twenties. The sometimes dangerous behaviour of adolescents can be blamed on immature prefrontal cortices – on overpowering curiosity rather than mischief.

It's a strange and baffling combination of capacities. Psychologists tend to divide the human psyche into intellect, emotions, and drives, and the major explanations of curiosity emphasise only one part of this trinity. But curiosity seems to issue from all three at once. As a result, none of the existing theories are entirely satisfactory.

One theory, dominant in the first half of the twentieth century, conceives of curiosity as a biological drive, like the urge to satisfy hunger or sexual desire. But instead of being satisfied by food or sex, the curiosity drive is satiated only by information. Just as we invest time and effort in acquiring the first two, the theory goes, we do the same with information, because humans need knowledge to survive and thrive. Sigmund Freud, to whom this theory can be traced, argued specifically that intellectual curiosity derives from the drive for sex.

This makes some intuitive sense; we speak about people being *driven* by curiosity, or having an *appetite* for knowledge. Curiosity, when we're in the grip of it, isn't always far from sexual desire — indeed the two can merge into voyeurism. The shortcoming of this theory is that it doesn't help to distinguish between the different kinds of knowledge people get interested in, from the sensory to the intellectual, the useful to the useless. Is the desire to know more about the religious rituals of Mayan civilisation really the same as the desire to know what Ryan Gosling looks like with his clothes off? The other problem with classifying curiosity this way is that it behaves differently to our other drives. When I finish a large meal, I may have no wish to eat again for a long time. But when I read an article on a topic I'm fascinated by, I immediately want to read more. Not being satisfied is what makes curiosity so satisfying.

The great developmental psychologist Jean Piaget framed curiosity as more of a cognitive activity, deriving from our deep intellectual need to make sense of the world. He proposed that a person's curiosity is provoked when she perceives an *incongruity* between what she expects and what happens – when she feels there's a discrepancy between what she thinks she knows, and what she sees. Piaget said that this helps us understand why children are bursting with curiosity and wonder – they are operating on a few, very simple theories about how the world works. Since much of what they witness every day doesn't fit those theories, nearly everything is a surprise, demanding explanation.

According to Piaget's theory, curiosity follows the curve of an inverted U, where the bottom axis represents the extent of our surprise:

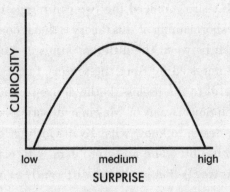

Curiosity is at its highest when the violation of an expectation is more than tiny and less than enormous. When violations are very minor we can quite easily ignore them. When they're massive, we often refuse to acknowledge them because we're scared of what they imply. Incongruity theory, however, doesn't explain why I try to overhear a conversation at the next table or why you have an enduring desire to learn as much as you can about the Crimean War.

In 1994, George Loewenstein, a psychologist and behavioural economist from Carnegie Mellon University, created a synthesis of these two approaches, the instinctual and the cognitive,. According to Loewenstein, curiosity is a response to an *information gap*. We feel curious where there is a gap between what we know and what we want to know. It's not just incongruity that evokes our desire to know, it's the absence of information. Information gaps often come in the form of questions: *What's in the box? Why is that man crying? What's a four letter word meaning 'suffering'?* You have some incomplete information – there is a box, there is a man crying, there is a crossword clue – and you want to find the missing part. Loewenstein's theory is deceptively simple, but it actually tells us something profound. To grasp it fully we need to know something about the thinker who most influenced Loewenstein's ideas about curiosity, Daniel Berlyne.

*

Born in Salford, near Manchester, in 1924, and educated at Cambridge, Daniel Berlyne spent most of his career as a psychologist in North America and continental Europe, including a year with Jean Piaget in Geneva. Berlyne was interested in why people get interested in things, and in particular why they get interested in 'the strange, the unusual, the puzzling'. In 1954, while at the University of Aberdeen, he published a paper that first made the seminal distinction between diversive and epistemic curiosity.

Berlyne exemplified both. He loved the thrill of exploration, physical and intellectual. During his adult life he moved from England to Scotland, to California, to Switzerland, Paris and Toronto. His research ranged across topics barely covered by his peers, like the psychology of artistic appreciation or humour. He was also a man of deep and enduring interests, as knowledgeable about Aristotle and Michelangelo as he was about Freud and Pavlov. He was fluent in six languages, and an avid collector of books, paintings, jokes and underground train journeys (one of his goals was to ride on every subway in the world).

Berlyne used to give his experimental subjects geometric shapes, like polygons, to look at. The shapes, and the patterns within them, would vary in complexity. He found that if people were presented with very simple shapes, they would barely glance at them before getting bored. They would spend more time gazing at the shapes if they were more complex. But if the patterns were extremely complex, people didn't spend much time on them either.

This very simple experiment illuminated a deep truth about curiosity, one that the cognitive psychologist Janet Metcalfe of Columbia University, who first told me about these experiments, described as 'beautiful and inspiring'. Berlyne had put his finger on a paradoxical attribute of curiosity — it is stimulated by understanding *and* by the absence of understanding. This tells us something important about the motivation to learn.

George Loewenstein built his 'information gap' theory out of Berlyne's insight. Information, he proposed, fuels curiosity by creating *awareness of ignorance*, which gives rise to a desire to know more. As soon as we know something about a subject, we start to become uncomfortably aware of what we *don't* know, and that makes us want to close the gap. William James anticipated Loewenstein when he said that 'scientific curiosity' (which corresponds closely to epistemic curiosity) arises from 'a gap in . . . knowledge, just as the musical brain responds to discord.' The crucial point here is that it's not simply the absence of information that creates curiosity, but a gap in our *existing* information:

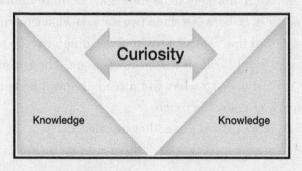

Curiosity is talked about as if it's a feeling that occurs when we don't know anything, and we often neglect the role that a little knowledge plays in stimulating it. People tend not to be curious about things of which they are completely ignorant. The German philosopher Ludwig Feuerbach remarked that 'man only wants to know what man can know. What lies beyond this region has no existence whatever for him; so for him it is also the object of no drive or wish whatsoever.' In his novel *In Search of Lost Time*, Marcel Proust described his protagonist Swann as lacking 'even the tiny, initial clue which, by allowing us to imagine what we do not know, stimulates a desire for knowledge.'

When we know nothing about a subject, we find it hard to engage our brains, either because we can't imagine finding it interesting, or because we're intimidated by the prospect of starting to learn about something that might, by its scale or complexity, defeat us. Conversely, when we know lots about a subject and feel that we have pretty much got it covered, we're unlikely to be interested in more information about it. In between these two states is what experts on learning call the 'zone of proximal learning'. For the sake of simplicity, I'll call it the curiosity zone. The curiosity zone is next door to what you already know, just before you feel you know too much.

It can be visualised as another inverted U:

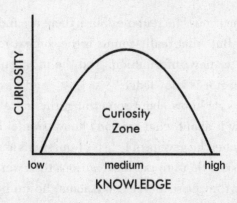

Thinking about curiosity like this helps us to distinguish between people who are truly incurious and people who only appear incurious because they don't have basic knowledge about the topic. If I tell you something about opera, and you know absolutely nothing about opera, you're unlikely to be interested in discussing it, which would also be the case if you think you already know everything there is to know about opera. But that doesn't make you an incurious person. Say that football is a topic you do know something about – you might suddenly get very curious if I then drop a fascinating fact about Manchester United into the conversation. Children and adults who are dismissed as incurious may be suffering from a different problem – a lack of basic information about the subject at hand.

Unless you're in the curiosity zone, it's very difficult to get interested in anything. George Loewenstein told me this is the most important implication of his theory. 'I don't believe in the idea that some people are really curious and others are really incurious,' he told me. 'Sure, there are individual differences. But what really counts is the context in which you encounter new information. And the most important contextual factor is knowledge.' *

The more we know about something, the more intense our curiosity is about what we *don't* know. Daniel Berlyne found that when he gave people lists of questions about animals, and asked them to rate how curious they were about the answers, they were most curious about the animals they already knew something about. Loewenstein points out that a person who knows the capitals of three out of thirty American states is likely to think of herself as knowing something ('I know three state capitals'). But a person who has learned the names of forty-seven state capitals is likely to think of herself *as not knowing* three state capitals. She's likely to *want* to learn those last three, and will make an effort to do so. Curiosity rises in tandem with knowledge.

The intensity of our curiosity is affected by whether we think the information that we're missing is likely to provide insight. After all, not all information is equal – sometimes, new information adds only a little to existing information; other times, it will throw light on an entire problem. Loewenstein describes a study in which subjects were sat in front

---

* This is one of the reasons that researchers find curiosity hard to measure; when presenting subjects with objects or topics about which they might or might not be curious, how do you account for their *prior* interests? Are you measuring their general level of curiosity or simply their curiosity about whatever it is you're presenting them with?

of computer screens that were divided into a grid of forty-five blank squares. Clicking on a square revealed a hidden image. In one condition, each square contained a different animal; in the other, each revealed part of what was one animal, filling the entire screen. Subjects in the first condition tended to get bored after realising that each square concealed a different animal. Those in the second condition were much more likely to keep clicking, because they wanted to comprehend the big picture.*

In order to feel curious – to feel the desire to close an information gap – you have to be aware that there is a gap in your knowledge in the first place. The trouble is, most of us, most of the time, go around thinking we know everything. Psychologists have demonstrated 'overconfidence effects' in many areas of our lives – most people think they're a better than average driver, or parent or lover. This is as true of the way we assess our own knowledge as it is of anything else; we're not very good at spotting our own information gaps, and that inclines us to be less curious than we ought to be.

In 1987, researchers at the University of Oklahoma ran

---

* Reading about this experiment made me think about the days when, as a single man, I used internet dating sites. If a person's profile didn't include a photo and offered only a cursory self-description I was unlikely to contact them. If it included several photos of them in varying outfits together with floridly detailed descriptions of their hobbies, hopes and dreams then I was equally likely to move on to the next profile. It was the profiles that offered just enough to intrigue – the face obscured by shadow, the self-description witty but elliptical – that compelled my curiosity.

an experiment in which they gave students a series of problems to solve, and asked them to generate as many solutions as they could. The researchers deliberately gave their subjects a very limited amount of information on each problem. One problem was how to provide enough parking spaces on the university campus, given the limited space available. The students came up with about three hundred solutions, in seven different categories, including reducing demand for parking space (by raising fees) or using the space more efficiently (by creating space for 'compact cars only').

After the students had generated their answer, they were asked to estimate what percentage of possible good solutions they thought they had come up with. Separately, a panel of experts had been asked to compile a database of the possible solutions. Understandably, given their efforts, the individuals guessed that they had landed on three out of four possible solutions. But when their answers were matched against the experts' database, it turned out that the average participant had generated only about one in three of the best solutions. The participants had missed most of the best ideas. Think of this as the 'ignorant but happy' effect – when people are confident that they have the answers they become blithely incurious about alternatives.

Loewenstein points out that this effect can help us understand our lazy assumptions in everyday life, like the way we tend to slot other people into stereotypes. I might assume that my taxi driver's conversation won't extend beyond the weather and the football; if I exercise my curiosity a little more I might find out about his PhD in sociology. Many bigoted assumptions can be explained by a failure to perceive the gaps in one's information. It's certainly a lot easier to go through life assuming you know everything that needs to be known. The Nobel prize-winning psychologist Daniel Kahneman puts it like this: 'Our comforting conviction the world makes sense rests on secure foundation: our almost unlimited ability to ignore our ignorance.'

If overconfidence undermines curiosity, so does a complete lack of confidence. As the psychologist Todd Kashdan puts it, 'anxiety and curiosity are two opposing systems.' Fear kills curiosity. Children who grow up in environments of profound physical or emotional uncertainty often seem to be incurious at school, but it's because they can't afford to concentrate on anything other than survival. They need to attend to who is on their side and who isn't, on how to avoid the worst from the grown-ups on whose care they depend, or with whose carelessness they are stuck. That takes up most of their cognitive resources, with little left over for playful exploration.

The dynamic between overconfidence and under confidence applies just as much to adult life. Take businesses, for example – firms in which employees live in fear of their jobs are unlikely to have environments conducive to curious thinking. Equally, firms in which employees feel that everything is going swimmingly and their bonuses are assured are also likely to see curiosity wither. Curiosity requires an edge of uncertainty to thrive; too much uncertainty and it freezes.

Thus we have our final inverted U:

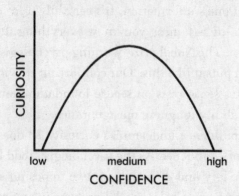

Curiosity has been called 'the knowledge emotion'. An information gap isn't just recognised rationally; its onset is like an itch that we have to scratch. Information gaps cause us pain, but it's a pain we invite in (in this sense, curiosity is fundamentally masochistic). In evolutionary terms, the primary role of emotions is motivational – anger makes us act to change a bad situation or right a wrong; love binds us to someone even when they disappoint us. The emotional force of curiosity is what impels us forward on our intellectual explorations even when there is no pressing need to do so, and keeps us enquiring even when we're weary or confused. A curious person knows that she won't feel emotionally fulfilled until she finds the information or the understanding she seeks. So she keeps reading or questioning until the gap is closed.

That's not to say that the curious person can ever feel completely satisfied. The philosopher John Stuart Mill, after suffering a childhood in which he was force-fed massive amounts of knowledge by his overbearing father (he was taught Greek at three), still managed to discover the pleasures of self-directed intellectual exploration as an adult. He held that, 'It is better to be a human being satisfied than a pig dissatisfied; better to be Socrates dissatisfied than a fool satisfied.' Curiosity is the sweetest form of dissatisfaction.

If curiosity is emotionally complex, that's because we are. Here is Leonardo da Vinci describing his investigation of a cave:

> I came to the entrance of a great cavern, in front of which I stood some time, astonished and unaware of such a thing. Bending my back into an arch I rested my left hand on my knee and held my right hand over my downcast and contracted eyebrows: often bending first one way and then the other, to see whether I could discover anything inside, and this being forbidden by the deep darkness within, and after having remained there some time, two contrary emotions arose in me, fear and desire – fear of the threatening dark cavern, desire to see whether there were any marvellous thing within it.

This is what being human entails. We spend our entire lives at the entrance of a cave, caught between the safety of the familiar and the yearning for novelty, the peace of home and the thrill of travel, the tonic and dominant chords. Toddlers in the park will wander off to explore, then run back to their parents, then venture away again. Our stories, from *The Odyssey* to *The Searchers* to Harry Potter, revolve around these two conflicting instincts – to strike out or stay home.

This brings us to another paradox – the more we love home, the more likely we are to strike out. In 1970, Mary Salter Ainsworth and Silvia Bell of Johns Hopkins University ran a series of experiments in which they would put a one-year-old child in a room with its mother and some toys. The mother left the room while the researchers watched how the child reacted to her departure. Then she returned, and this was the part that Salter Ainsworth and Bell were really interested in. The infants with a 'secure attachment' to their mother greeted her joyfully, before returning to their exploration of the room and its toys.

Those with a more troubled relationship also greeted their mother's return, but were then much less likely to return to their explorations, as if fearful that if they turned their backs again, their mother would disappear. In Susan Engel's summary of the study's findings, 'insecure children are less likely to make physical and psychological expeditions to gather information.' Curiosity is underwritten by love.

Information gaps make good bait. When you read about a murder and you don't know who committed it, your curiosity is aroused. The information – Mr Ratchett has been stabbed to death on the Orient Express – engages your attention. The gap – nobody knows who did it – sucks you in. You've learned something, which makes you want to know more, and, in the hands of a master storyteller like Agatha Christie, this sets up a magnetic current of curiosity that pulls you through the rest of the book.

In the early years of the last decade I lived and worked in New York, where I was lucky enough to attend a seminar given by the great Robert McKee, the godfather of screenwriting teachers. Just about every successful screenwriter, and many more unsuccessful ones, have sat in one of McKee's classes or read his magnum opus, *Story*. For two days, a cantankerous white-haired man with a rasping, cigarette-burned voice held an audience of hundreds spellbound, speaking largely without notes or props. McKee spoke about what distinguishes a good movie from a bad one, and, more specifically, the fundamental structure of great stories. Sure, said McKee, a movie can have amazing special effects or deep existential ideas, but it will only be great if it rests on the foundation of a well-constructed story.

Stories depend on the artful manipulation of what Loewenstein calls information gaps. In McKee's words, 'Curiosity is the intellectual need to answer questions and close open patterns. Story plays to this universal desire by doing the opposite, posing questions and opening situations.' The storyteller plays a cat and mouse game with the viewer (or reader, or listener), opening and closing information gaps as the narrative unfolds, unspooling the viewer's curiosity. According to McKee, every scene in a movie should be a

Turning Point: 'Each Turning Point hooks curiosity. The audience wonders, *What will happen next?*, and *How will it turn out?*'*

'What will happen next?' is a question that can pin us to our chairs, raise our heartbeats and make us sweat. Alfred Hitchcock was expert at creating painful information gaps in the minds of his viewers, consisting precisely of this question. He was a perfect judge of just how much his viewers should be allowed to know in any given scene, and what should be withheld from them. He turned their curiosity into a thumbscrew. One of his maxims was, 'Always make the audience suffer as much as possible'. Hitchcock was an information sadist.

You can take the opening scene of any movie and identify the information it gives you and the gaps it leaves. In *Citizen Kane*, for instance, we learn that a millionaire tycoon has died, and that his last word was 'Rosebud'. We are left to wonder what Rosebud refers to, and why it's so significant, until the end. Sometimes, information gaps are the whole point of the narrative, as in a murder mystery. At other times they are introduced to generate momentum so that the storyteller can explore his wider themes. Alfred Hitchcock called his information gaps 'McGuffins' – simple devices that moved his plots along.

---

* 'How will it turn out?' is such a powerful question that it can keep your eyes glued to the screen *even when you're not enjoying the movie*. It keeps us turning the pages of a mediocre novel or watching a poorly made soap opera. We seem to have this inherent curiosity about how things will unfold, even things we care little about.

Puzzles and Mysteries

The best storytellers in any form are artful shapers of the narrative equivalent of what designers call 'negative space' – the shapes that lie between what is visible. George Orwell economically sculpts an information gap with the opening sentence of *Nineteen Eighty-Four*: 'It was a bright cold day in April, and the clocks were striking thirteen.' You want to read on to find out why the clocks work differently in this world. In some stories, an information gap is deliberately left unclosed at the end. Just what did Bill Murray whisper to Scarlett Johansson in *Lost in Translation*? What is it that Meatloaf won't do for love?

It's not just artists who use information gaps this way. Advertisers are fond of teaser campaigns, in which unbranded ads are used to stoke the curiosity of consumers before the main campaign reveals what it's all about. In the workplace, skilful presenters will often start by posing a question to the people in the room that they only answer fully after exploring several alternatives; when the presenter finally arrives at the answer, her audience are then more likely to believe it's the right one, because they're experiencing the emotional satisfaction of closing an information gap. Some people are expert users of information gaps in conversation – they might refer in passing to the time they met Fidel Castro, knowing that until they close that gap, they have you hooked.

You may be thinking that some of these tricks might be more likely to annoy you than interest you. You may also wonder whether Agatha Christie is the highest example of the storyteller's art, or whether stories, and the curiosity they arouse, can serve deeper purposes. To a certain extent, the irritation created by a narrative trick or a teaser campaign is beside the point if the author has made you read on or notice his product. But I'd say your annoyance is significant, because it points to a gap in Loewenstein's theory of information gaps. Curiosity is about more than the hunt for missing information.

Loewenstein's definition of curiosity is powerful, but it's even more useful with a modification. He proposes that curiosity is about finding the answer in order to salve our frustration at the gap where the information should be. But when we come upon a field of knowledge that we feel sure will occupy us for a long time to come, whether it's neuroscience or languages, it's because we know we'll never get to the end of our ignorance. That feeling isn't uncomfortable or, as the psychologists say, 'aversive'. It is enormously affirming, something like the confidence you (ought to) feel when you ask your partner to marry you. It's a very different feeling to one you get when you're trying to fill out the last clue in a crossword puzzle. So what kind of curiosity is this?

The security and intelligence expert Gregory Treverton once made a very useful distinction between puzzles and mysteries. Puzzles have definite answers. When you're trying to answer that crossword clue, you know the kind of answer you need, even if you don't know what it is yet. Even when you don't know the answer, you know the question, and you know that a corresponding answer exists. Puzzles are orderly; they have a beginning and an end. Once the missing information is found, it's not a puzzle anymore. The frustration you felt when you were searching for the answer is replaced by satisfaction.

Mysteries are murkier, less neat. They pose questions that can't be answered definitively, because the answers often depend on a highly complex and interrelated set of factors, both known and unknown. They tend to involve slippery concepts like public opinion and human psychology. Progress can be made towards solving them by gathering knowledge and identifying the most important factors. But they don't offer the satisfaction of definite solutions. The problem here isn't an information gap, necessarily – indeed, sometimes the problem is that there is too much information – but in knowing which information is important and which isn't, and how to interpret the information you have.

Puzzles tend to be *how many* or *where* questions; mysteries are more likely to be *why* or *how*. Treverton was writing about how the job of US intelligence had changed since the era of the Cold War, when America's spies and analysts were tasked mainly with solving puzzles: How many missiles did the Soviet Union possess? Where were they? How fast could they travel? But with the collapse of the Soviet Union and the rise of global terrorism, the primary task of intelligence became to define the most important mysteries.[*]

We have a tendency to prioritise puzzles over mysteries, because we know they can be solved. The question 'Where is Osama Bin Laden?' was a puzzle, and when it was solved there was great jubilation. 'How best to combat Islamist terrorism?', arguably a much more important question, is a mystery, but it receives far less attention among the public and in the media because it is so complex and seemingly intractable. Treverton suggests that if US intelligence had treated the question of Saddam's Iraq not as a puzzle ('Does Iraq possess WMD?') but as a mystery ('What is Saddam thinking?') then it might have landed on the insight that Saddam was boasting about weapons he didn't have.

I think this distinction has applications far beyond the field of national security. Puzzles and mysteries correspond to different types of curiosity. To illustrate this, let's return to stories. Agatha Christie constructed puzzles, in which a key piece of information – the identity of the murderer – is withheld until the end (in this sense, the term 'murder mystery' is a misnomer). The reader's desire to discover who committed the murder is transient – when he finds out that it was Colonel Barker with strychnine, he gains the pleasure of discovery but, at the same moment, his curiosity dies.

---

[*] Psychologists talk about 'specific curiosity' – the desire to find a specific piece of information; a jigsaw piece. Puzzles and mysteries correspond roughly with specific and epistemic curiosity.

The curiosity inspired by, say, *The Great Gatsby* is of a different order. It is deeper and longer lived. It invites you to ponder questions which have no definite answer: What kind of a man is Gatsby? What is the meaning of the green light? What is the true nature of the American dream? The reader, or viewer, can return to these stories, and these questions, over and over, their curiosity engaged but never sated. F. Scott Fitzgerald's novels sell fewer copies than Agatha Christie's. But they offer more profound satisfactions.

Truly ambitious artists are more interested in mysteries than puzzles. One way of describing the achievement of the TV series *The Wire* was that it took a genre, the police procedural, which is conventionally based on puzzles, in the form of crimes that are solved each week, and turned it into a mystery – the mystery of Baltimore's crime problem. (And in doing so it demonstrated that while police and politicians like to present urban crime as a puzzle with a definite answer – Arrest all the users! Longer prison sentences! – it is more akin to a mystery: multi-layered, shifting, nuanced.)

Earlier I mentioned the role that 'Rosebud' plays in *Citizen Kane*. Its introduction at the beginning of the movie creates an information gap, because it seems to be the key that will explain Kane's life to us. When, at the end of the film, the gap is closed – Rosebud was Kane's childhood sleigh – we feel disappointed, because it doesn't really seem to explain anything. Orson Welles knew what he was doing. He was playing with the conventions of popular narratives, which rely on puzzles to manipulate the reader or viewer's attention. Welles was suggesting that a man's inner life is a mystery, not a puzzle, and that the meaning of a life is a question to which there are no easy answers.

In his book *Will in the World*, the literary scholar Stephen Greenblatt identifies a key turning point in the artistic evolution of William Shakespeare. Up until the mid-1590s Shakespeare was happy to adapt conventional storylines to his own ends, borrowing his plots from legends and chronicles. But at a certain point – Greenblatt connects it to the death of the playwright's beloved son, Hamnet – Shakespeare started to take these older narrative structures and remove crucial planks from them, in a way that made it harder for his audience to understand why his characters acted the way they did. It was as if he had lost faith in the comprehensibility of the universe and he wanted his own stories to reflect that. In Greenblatt's words, 'the principle was not the making of a riddle, but the creation of a strategic opacity'.

Take the play considered by many to be Shakespeare's greatest – *Hamlet* was based on an ancient Scandinavian legend. Shakespeare took this old story and made a crucial change to the plot. In the original version it is public knowledge that the prince's father was murdered by the current king. Amleth, the prince, is therefore expected to avenge his father's killer. But Amleth is very young, a boy, and needs to bide his time. So he feigns madness as a way of avoiding the attentions of the king's henchmen while he makes plans for revenge. In Shakespeare's version, our hero is already a young man, and the murder is a secret, revealed exclusively to Hamlet by his father's ghost.

Hamlet's feigned madness, and his delay, are therefore entirely unnecessary, and not easy to understand or explain. As a consequence, Shakespeare's Hamlet still fascinates us centuries later, while Amleth is forgotten, despite being more easily understood – actually, *because* he is more easily understood. Mysteries have a longer half-life than puzzles.

Great scientists and inventors think in terms of mysteries rather than puzzles too; they are more interested in uncertainty than certainty. The physicist Freeman Dyson has remarked that science is not a collection of truths, but 'a continuing exploration of mysteries'. Ray Dolby, the American inventor and audio pioneer, eloquently expresses how this principle applies to innovation: 'To be an inventor, you have to be willing to live with a sense of uncertainty, to work in the darkness and grope toward an answer, to put up with the anxiety about whether there *is* an answer.' It's a sentiment Albert Einstein would have recognised. 'The most beautiful thing we can experience is the mysterious,' said Einstein. 'It is the source of all true art and science.'*

---

* Even puzzles can be divided into puzzles and mysteries. In a 2012 interview with CNN, Erno Rubik, who gave the world the Rubik's Cube, reflected on the success of his invention, and in particular its ability to captivate the user even after it has been 'solved': 'It's not something like a jigsaw puzzle where you start to work on it, spend some time on it, and in the end it's solved, it's finished. If you find a solution with the cube, it doesn't mean you find everything. It's only a starting point. You can work on and find something else, you can improve your solution, you can make it shorter, you can go deeper and deeper and collect knowledge and many other things.' This is a perfect articulation of the distinction between a puzzle and a mystery.

We live in a culture that is keener on puzzles than mysteries. In school and even at university, science is presented as a series of questions corresponding with neatly defined answers, rather than, as Dyson would have it, the rigorous and persistent exploration of what we don't know. Politicians tend to think of education policy as a puzzle, in which the aim is to match inputs (teaching) with specific outputs (jobs); indeed they present all of society's complex problems as if they are puzzles with simple answers. The media like to turn life into a series of puzzles that can be solved by watching a programme, or buying a book or a product ('You have Problem X? You need Y'). Business people prefer to frame their problems as puzzles, because puzzles and their solutions are more easily articulated in a few bullet points on a PowerPoint chart, and more easily measured. Google can give us the powerful illusion that all questions have definite answers.

We need to resist this cultural pressure. Puzzles offer us the satisfaction of answering a question even while you're missing the point completely. A society or an organisation that thinks only in terms of puzzles is one that is too focused on the goals it has set, rather than on the possibilities it can't yet see. A person who thinks of every problem in their life as a puzzle will feel confused and frustrated at the way some questions just don't resolve themselves into simple answers (despite what the self-help gurus tell him). Mysteries are more challenging, but more sustaining. They inspire long-term curiosity by keeping us focused on what we don't know.

They keep us feeling 'alive and active' even as we work in the darkness.

In the final assignment of third grade, Jack was asked to research the anaconda. After spending three hours on the internet he produced a detailed report on the animal, dense with facts. It touched on the snake's habitat (semi-aquatic), prey (includes goats and ponies) and size (massive).

Jack was proud of his report, and after presenting it to his teacher he brought it to his father to read. 'It's the largest snake in the world,' he told his father. His father replied with a question: 'What's the second-largest snake in the world?' Jack frowned slightly. Then he turned away, walked back to his bedroom, and started tapping at his computer keyboard. Within a minute, he came back and told his father the answer.

This little exchange is not particularly remarkable; versions of it take place thousands of times a day in households across the world. In any home with an internet connection, questions are answered with the assistance of Google and Wikipedia. Indeed, the only reason we know about this one is that Jack's father is the writer Ben Greenman, who wrote about it for the *New York Times*. Greenman felt it said something about difference between the way his son acquires knowledge and the way that he did as a child.

About a month after the anaconda conversation with his son, Greenman picked up the 'S' volume of an old encyclopaedia and turned to the page on snakes. He read information he knew already – that snakes are reptiles – and information he didn't – that most snakes have only one functional lung. What the encyclopaedia entry on snakes didn't tell him was what the second-biggest snake was. He read closely, but there was no search function, and no 'second-largest' entry.

Greenman reflected that if he'd been asked the question when he was a child he might, after a fruitless search in his family's encyclopedia, have been motivated enough to visit the library and check out a book on snakes. More likely, though, he would have got on with his life in third and later fourth grade, faintly feeling the itch of the unanswered question at the back of his mind.

The internet's ability to scratch such itches in an instant is, Greenman argues, a mixed blessing:

> By supplying answers to questions with such ruthless efficiency, the internet cuts off the supply of an even more valuable commodity: productive frustration. Education, at least as I remember it, isn't only, or even primarily, about creating children who are proficient with information. It's about filling them with questions that ripen, via deferral, into genuine interests.

Greenman eloquently describes the way that the internet closes information gaps, and, by doing so, forecloses curiosity. It has a tendency to turn mysteries into puzzles, and puzzles into instantly answered questions. Our children are used to finding definitive answers to even the most indeterminate questions, like 'What is beauty?' The web solves the puzzles for us before we've had a chance to flex our cognitive muscles. As a result, we can allow them to waste away.

We've seen how storytellers artfully withhold information, priming the pump of curiosity by planting questions in the reader or viewer's mind. When someone tells you how your favourite TV series is going to end, you get angry, because the pleasurable frustration of *not knowing* has been taken away from you. The same applies to our intellectual journeys – answers, when they are too easily available, kill curiosity before it has a chance to take root. Since Greenman wrote his piece, Google has only become more efficient; its searches now often provide the answer to your query on the Google results page, so you don't even have to venture into another website. A Google murder mystery would tell you the name of the murderer on page one – actually, before page one. Google is the ultimate spoiler.

J.J. Abrams, the film and television producer who created *Lost* and reinvigorated the *Star Trek* franchise, expressed his concerns about what he calls the 'age of immediacy' in an article for *Wired* magazine:

Mystery, obviously, is everywhere. Is there a God? Mystery. What about life after death? Mystery. Excuse me, what material is the ShamWow made of? Mystery. Stonehenge? Big Foot? Loch Ness? Mystery mystery mystery . . . And yet: For all that mystery, why does it feel like the world has been ripped open, all parts exposed? Why does so much seem abso-

*lutely and thoroughly demystified? These days we can leap,
all of us, from a casual curiosity about anything to a sense
of satisfying understanding. Instantly. Want to fold origami?
There are more than 200,000 Google results on that subject
available to you, now. Need to know the capital of Mauri-
tania? A recipe for sticky buns? How to pick a bicycle lock?
You could answer all these questions in less time than it will
take you to finish reading this article.*

But mystery, says Abrams, 'demands that you stop and consider – or, at the very least, slow down and discover.'

So does difficulty – the world's resistance to our desires.
Technology makes it easier for us to build shelters, travel,
hunt, grow and prepare food, extract energy from the
ground and the air, communicate across distances, and wash
the dishes. The very reason we have technology is to make
things easier. But making things easier can come at a cost –
there can be hidden value in difficulty. It's a principle that
seems to apply with special force to the way we learn. The
harder things are to grasp or memorise, the more our brains
rise to the challenge.

Abraham Lincoln was an autodidact who made himself
erudite in literature, history and the law. He wasn't the
quickest learner, however. If you had been at school with
him, you probably wouldn't have marked him out as a future
lawyer, let alone a future president. A cousin remembers
him as 'somewhat dull . . . not a brilliant boy, but worked
his way by toil.' Lincoln himself remarked that 'I am slow

to learn and slow to forget that which I have learned. My mind is like a piece of steel, very hard to scratch anything on it but almost impossible after you get it there to rub it out."* Lincoln's phrase – 'slow to learn and slow to forget' – actually describes a universal truth about the way our brains absorb information. In the early 1990s, a cognitive scientist at the University of California called Robert Bjork landed upon an insight that changed the way psychologists think about learning. In its simplest form, it is this: we learn better when we find learning difficult.

We tend to assume that learning things easily is the same as learning them well; teachers are pleased when children grasp a concept or a skill in one lesson, and so, of course, are children. The trouble is, when learning is too easy, we may not actually be learning much at all. In a series of carefully designed experiments, Bjork showed that when people learn something rapidly they often learn it superficially; that is, they are more liable to forget it in the long term. They are also less likely to integrate the new information with what they already know, which means

---

* Winston Churchill was an even poorer performer at school. He came bottom of his class at Harrow and was made to repeat a year three times. But he later reflected that his time spent in the lowest form gave him an advantage, because he spent so long doing boring, repetitive drills in English grammar that he learned it deeply and ineradicably: 'Thus I got into my bones the essential structure of the ordinary British sentence – which is a noble thing.' Much later, of course, he was to put this hard-earned knowledge to work in a way that changed the course of history.

the new knowledge is less 'transferable' — that is, applicable to other problems.

In one experiment, students were asked to study a passage of text with the aim of remembering it. Before reading it, one group was given an outline that summarised the information in the same order as the text, while another group was given an outline that put the same information in a different order. Participants in the first group appeared to learn the text better — they scored higher on a test of recall. But when the two groups were set creative problem-solving tasks related to the text — the kind of tasks that required a deeper understanding of its content — it was the second group who came out on top. The extra difficulty faced by the second group in comprehending the text made it more difficult to recall, but increased their understanding of what it was about. That meant they were better equipped to transfer their knowledge to the creative problems.

Psychologists at Princeton and Indiana universities found that students remembered reading material better when it was printed in an ugly, difficult-to-read font.* Scientists from the University of Amsterdam set people anagram puzzles to solve, while, as an obstacle to concentration, a series of random numbers were read out. Compared with those in a control group who performed the same task without this distraction, these subjects displayed greater cognitive agility

---

* The paper is entitled 'Fortune favors the **bold** (and the *italicized*): effects of disfluency on educational outcomes.' Emphasis in the original.

— they were more likely to take leaps of association and make unusual connections. The researchers also found that when people are forced to cope with unexpected obstacles they react by increasing their 'perceptual scope' — taking a mental step back to see the bigger picture. When you find your journey to work blocked by a construction site, you have to map the city in your mind.

Robert Bjork coined the phrase 'desirable difficulties' to describe the counter-intuitive notion that we learn better when the learning is hard. His work has influenced thinking on education; he recommends, for instance, spacing teaching sessions further apart so that students have to make more effort to recall what they learned last time. Difficulty is desirable when it comes to human information processing (or 'learning' in normal language) because it forces our brain to work harder at encoding and integrating the inputs that it has coming in. It makes us think, and the harder we think, the better we remember. The same applies to anything we can get better at. Skills come from struggle.

Reading books or talking to experts may be harder, take more time, and be more frustrating than Google searches. But that's exactly why we learn more and learn deeper by doing so. Wikipedia is an amazingly powerful tool for learning, used in the right way. If you are investigating, say, medieval cathedral architecture, or the invention of the scanner, and you use Wikipedia to get an overview of the subject, or as a gateway to other source materials, you are exercising your epistemic curiosity. But if you depend on

Wikipedia as a source of easy answers you will be degrading your capacity to learn.

You may also come to find that you lose interest in questions that can't be easily answered. 'To search' used to mean embarking on an arduous quest. It implied a question that led to more questions. You would encounter obstacles, or get lost, and you might not even find what you were started out looking for, but you would learn something along the way. Your perceptual scope – your mental map – would have increased. Now, a search means typing a word or two into a box, or muttering them into a mouthpiece, and getting an answer almost instantaneously.

Google wants to delete that 'almost'. In an interview given in 2004, Google's founders, Larry Page and Sergey Brin, described their ambition: 'Search will be included in people's brains,' said Page. 'When you think about something and you don't really know much about it, you will automatically get information.' All information gaps will be closed. 'Ultimately,' said Brin, 'I view Google as a way to augment your brain with knowledge of the world.' Page summed up their vision: 'You'll have the implant, where if you think about a fact, it will just tell you the answer.' Google aims to save you from the itch of curiosity altogether.

In a 2012 interview with the *Guardian*, Google's head of search, Amit Singhal explained Google's goal in terms similar to Page and Brin: 'We are maniacally focusing on the user to reduce every possible friction point between them, their thoughts and the information they want to find.'

Singhal's devotion to this mission is good for Google but not necessarily good for human curiosity, which *depends* on friction, on the struggle to close information gaps, on uncertainty, mystery and the awareness of ignorance.

We're becoming so used to easy answers that we're forgetting how to ask questions. The *Guardian* asked Singhal if his efforts to refine Google's accuracy are being boosted as users learn how to enter search terms with greater precision. 'Actually,' Singhal replied, with a weary sigh, 'it works the other way. The more accurate the machine gets, the lazier the questions become.'

PART TWO
THE CURIOSITY DIVIDE

CHAPTER 4

Three Ages of Curiosity

*From this disease of curiosity are all those strange sights
exhibited in the theatre.*

St Augustine

The Age of Danger

The way we think about curiosity has been anything but
stable. As George Loewenstein puts it, curiosity has been
subject to 'epochal attitude swings' – in some eras regarded
as a vice, in others a virtue, and in our own a confusing mix
of both. Its chequered past helps to explain the disparate,
conflicting ways we use the words 'curiosity' and 'curious'
today. Other than describing someone with a hunger for
knowledge, we also use 'curious' to mean strange or weird,
or to hint at danger. In the very ambiguity of the term is
written its, well, curious history.

In ancient Athens, curiosity, or *curiositas*, meant the

pursuit of knowledge purely for its own sake. Men investigated the world and made theories about it because it was interesting, said Aristotle, 'not for any utilitarian end'. The Greeks believed that if it wasn't a waste of time, it wasn't worth doing. If knowledge could be put to practical use, that was all very well, but to start with such an aim was rather grubby. Curiosity's only end was the elevation of the soul. In the words of the historian Hans Blumenburg, 'what theory was supposed to do was not to make life possible but to make it happy.' The Greeks found their happiness in the free play of debate, experiment and investigation. *Idle* curiosity – 'reposeful and bliss-conferring contemplation' – was the only game in Athens.

The Romans inherited this purist conception of curiosity. Cicero defined it as 'an innate love of learning and of knowledge . . . without the lure of any profit.' It wasn't a purely cerebral pursuit; it was something deeply felt. Cicero called curiosity the 'passion for knowing', and argued that Ulysses was drawn to the Sirens because they promised to satisfy his vast intellectual curiosity, rather than his sexual desire (though, frankly, that was probably just Cicero). Curiosity was also talked about as a bodily urge – an 'appetite'. It embodied our lowest and highest desires.

As the Catholic Church asserted its dominance over the lives of Europeans, the reputation of curiosity suffered a centuries-long reversal. The key figures in early Christianity regarded *curiositas* as a sinful diversion from the only object worthy of contemplation: God. In his *Confessions*,

Saint Augustine identified three problems with curiosity. First, it was, at least in the way Greeks conceived of it, pointless; curiosity prompted men to investigate things that are 'useless to know, but which people desire to know only for the sake of knowing.' Second, it was perverted. Just as lust overwhelmed the body and diverted men from the path of righteousness, so curiosity waylaid the mind; Augustine himself wrote of being distracted from his prayers by his curiosity about a passing lizard or a spider catching flies (luckily for him, he never had to cope with Twitter). Third, it was prideful; man's desire to see or know what was hidden from him was an arrogant usurpation of divine authority. Why should he seek knowledge that God had not seen fit to present him with?

Some nine hundred years after Augustine laid down the law, Thomas Aquinas became the first major Church figure to challenge the orthodox view of curiosity. Though he insisted that it should only have one ultimate purpose – a greater understanding of God – Aquinas was a little more sympathetic to the Aristotelian desire for knowledge of the world. He made an important distinction between two types of curiosity. The first – the sinful kind – was half-hearted, aimless, quickly satisfied and transient, 'a superficial dwelling on the object' (pretty much St Augustine's view of curiosity). The second kind was one that sought 'knowledge of truth about the Creation.' This type of curiosity was studious and serious. (As you'll have noted, this is similar to the distinction between diversive and epistemic curiosity.)

Aquinas proposed a simple but powerful argument against the strict Augustinian view of curiosity: 'However much it abounds, knowledge of the truth is not bad, but good.'

Curiosity retained its bad reputation throughout the medieval period, however. It was only in the fifteenth century, with the revival of interest in classical ideas which came to be known as the Renaissance, that curiosity started to become respectable again – or, if not quite respectable, at least glamorous. The dashing genius Leonardo da Vinci embodied a new and daring interest in the unknown, unexamined and prohibited. The Church's monopoly on learning came into conflict with a growing political, military and economic impetus to investigate, understand and ultimately gain dominion over the natural world, a tension that came to a climax in the trial of Galileo, who first became a hero for demonstrating that the earth revolved around the sun, and then a prisoner for insisting it was the truth.

Galileo's imprisonment was a rearguard action; the Church was fighting a losing battle. Great thinkers, backed by powerful patrons like the Medicis, were transforming humanity's view of its place in the universe. Galileo's telescope and, later, the news of Newton's orderly cosmos, opened up new and very practical possibilities in the realms of war, exploration and trade. The Protestant Reformation had loosened the grip of Catholic dogma, making it more acceptable to question orthodoxies. In the seventeenth century, worldly curiosity was adopted by Europe's ruling classes. As barriers to travel and information dissolved, traders, administrators and soldiers were bringing back amazing tales and glittering treasures from exotic lands, at the same time as scientists were proposing new theories of how the earth turned.

The 'curiosity cabinet' embodied a new conception of the globe and the cosmos beyond as a mystery that demanded exploration – a mystery of complex, terrifying, gorgeous variety. Otherwise known as *Wunderkammeren* (wonder rooms), these glass-fronted cabinets might contain rubies, Eastern sculptures, 'unicorn' horns, pocket watches, pistols, astrolabes, miniature paintings, perfume bottles, deadly poisons, fossils, relics, silk ribbons, Amazonian drugs, bezoar stones. The objects could be from nature or man-made, instantly appealing or compellingly weird. But they were all, in their way, displays of knowledge, and a way to signal status. In societies where commerce was making commoners rich, it was becoming ever more important to be seen to be educated and humane. The curiosity cabinet was a way of saying: 'Look – scientific know-how, refined cultural tastes, technological expertise, and a witty sensibility – I contain *all this*.' It was an elaborately constructed selfie.

Not long after it became clear that curiosity was useful, it started to become virtuous again. In 1620, Sir Francis Bacon reassured his readers that Adam and Eve had sinned by seeking moral knowledge, rather than knowledge of nature, and that God regarded scientific investigation as an 'innocent and kindly sport of children playing at hide-and-seek'. Rather than being a raid on a forbidden realm, the investigation of nature was reframed as a way of further revealing the glory of God's creation, a sign of humanity's superiority to the animals.

If the Renaissance, global trade and the scientific revolution made curiosity respectable again, it was the printing press that made it popular.

The Age of Questions

Society is held together by communication and information.

Samuel Johnson

In the sixteenth century, a bottom-up revolution in what one historian has called 'the mental operation of men' got underway, powered by an extraordinary new technology. Gutenberg's printing press was a curiosity machine. It facilitated the rapid spread and exchange of ideas, corroding old certainties and igniting powerful new ideas. Its significance was already apparent early in the seventeenth century – Sir Francis Bacon called the printing press one of three inventions, along with firearms and the compass, that 'changed the whole face and state of the world'.

Bacon proclaimed it time for a 'total reconstruction of sciences, arts, and all human knowledge'. The new knowledge, he argued, must be built not on the further refinement of abstract principles but on *observation*. Ian Morris, the historian, paraphrases Bacon's advice: 'Philosophers should get their noses out of books and look instead at the things all around them – stars and insects, cannons and oars, falling apples and wobbling chandeliers.' They should also talk to the people who knew how things worked: 'blacksmiths, clockmakers and mechanics'.

In the eighteenth century, Bacon's manifesto became a reality in a way not even he had foreseen. The blacksmiths, clockmakers and mechanics themselves became natural philosophers. Science went from being a monkish hoarding of knowledge to an exciting pursuit ordinary people could practise and enjoy. In Britain it became fashionable to be an amateur inventor, to write reports of birdwatching expeditions on local moors, to tinker with chemistry sets, or form discussion groups in homes and coffee houses on the great issues of the day.*

As literacy rates rose, the British embarked on a mass cognitive adventure. According to the historian Roy Porter, between 1660 and 1800 over 300,000 separate book and pamphlet titles were published in England, amounting to something like 200 million copies. The presses churned out

---

* Here's the historian Matthew Green on the eighteenth-century London coffee house: 'Unexpectedly wide-ranging discussions could be twined from a single conversational thread as when, at John's coffee house in 1715, news about the execution of a rebel Jacobite Lord . . . transmogrified into a discourse on "the ease of death by beheading" with one participant telling of an experiment he'd conducted slicing a viper in two and watching in amazement as both ends slithered off in different directions. Was this, as some of the company conjectured, proof of the existence of two consciousnesses?'

teach-yourself guides, educational treatises and advice man-
uals on anything from gardening to gymnastics, carpentry
to cookery. Reference books like Johnson's *Dictionary* and
the *Encyclopaedia Britannica* were published, along with
histories of the arts and sciences.

The birth of a thriving newspaper industry also galvan-
ised minds and generated questions; by the 1770s there were
nine London dailies and fifty local weeklies, and twelve
million newspapers were sold annually. 'Knowledge is dif-
fused among our people by the news-papers,' said Samuel
Johnson. The historian Charles Tanford has written that
the Age of Enlightenment was not so much about *being*
enlightened as *becoming* enlightened: 'Anyone who chose
to exercise his brain and powers of observation could learn
something new about almost any subject'. All you had to do
was ask someone where to look.

Not everyone welcomed these developments. Alexander
Catcott, a grumpy anti-Newtonian, noticed that people were
getting ideas above their station: 'Every man in this Enlightened age (having been fully instructed by those genteel
and easy conveyances of knowledge, newspapers and maga-
zines)' presumed to have 'the liberty of making a philosophy
(and I might add indeed a religion) for himself.' Catcott had
spotted something – the new knowledge was empowering,
and the curiosity it inspired was subversive. Reading Locke's
philosophy of human rights, or reading news of the revolution in France, made a person more likely to question the
fairness of his society. Such questions would lead, eventually,

to the great social and political reforms of the nineteenth century.

If Britain's rulers feared where all this questioning would end up, they also saw that it was bringing tangible rewards. Epistemic curiosity was the intellectual steam power of Britain's industrial revolution. The economic historian Joel Mokyr uses the term 'industrial enlightenment' to describe the way Britain's economic growth was fuelled by ideas and knowledge, rather than just natural resources. The leading figures of the age were flamboyantly curious and highly entrepreneurial. Benjamin Franklin, James Watt and Erasmus Darwin weren't intellectuals in ivory towers, but swashbuckling figures who wanted to change the world rather than merely contemplate it. They became iconic figures in their own lifetime; Franklin, in particular, was fixed in the public mind by the image of him capturing lightning with his kite. These were men who took ostentatious delight in learning, questioning and arguing around the dinner table or in a coffee house. They made curiosity cool.

It is hardly possible to overstate the value in the present state of human improvement of placing human beings in contact with other persons dissimilar to themselves, and with modes of thought and action unlike those with which they are familiar.

John Stuart Mill

In parallel with the rise of epistemic curiosity, another kind of curiosity was burgeoning – curiosity about the thoughts and feelings of others, including those very different from oneself. Of course, being interested in what others are up to is a fundamental part of being human; we are a nosy species, compelled to observe and learn from those around us. But from the eighteenth century onwards the desire to understand the minds and dispositions of people very different from oneself became more urgent, and the ability to do so more honed.

The new locus of curiosity was not the drawing room, but the street. To borrow from Jane Jacobs, the rise of the city provided 'what otherwise could be given only by travelling; namely, the strange.' Strangers, a rare phenomenon if you lived in a village, were everywhere in the city, and their strangeness invited investigation, or at least speculation. In the room downstairs, or just around the corner, were secret passions, bizarre beliefs, weird customs. Like many of his contemporaries, James Boswell didn't like the way cities packed people together, but Samuel Johnson saw it as a strength: 'It is not in the showy evolutions of buildings, but in the multiplicity of human habitations which are crowded together, that the wonderful immensity of London consists.' Johnson's most famous remark – 'When a man is tired of London, he is tired of life' – captured the sense of the city as a mystery that could never be exhausted.

The major index of the rise in *empathic* curiosity was literature: fiction, drama and poetry. William Shakespeare was born in the same year as Galileo Galilei (1564). Each might be considered founding figures of, respectively, empathic and epistemic curiosity. Around the same time as Sir Francis Bacon — another founding figure — codified the scientific method, Shakespeare revolutionised the dramatic soliloquy, allowing ordinary men and women a glimpse inside the minds and hearts of kings.

In the eighteenth century, a whole new literary form was born; the novel took readers further inside the consciousness of others than any previous kind of story. There proved to be a tremendous popular hunger for such journeys. Daniel Defoe's *Robinson Crusoe* (1719) had a print run of 5,000 in its first year; Henry Fielding's *Amelia* (1751) sold as many in its first week. This desire to read about the lives of others went far beyond nosiness. When readers picked up *Pamela* or *David Copperfield* they were finding out something of what it felt like to *be* another person — to spend time inside the mind of someone from a different sex, age, culture or class. In 1759 the economist and philosopher Adam Smith argued that each of us can be a 'judicious spectator' who imagines as vividly as possible what it is to be 'in the situation of the other', and he used literary reading as his model for this new way of thinking. A hundred years later, the novelist George Eliot proposed that, 'the greatest benefit we owe the artist, whether painter, poet or novelist, is the extension of our sympathies.'

The contemporary American philosopher Richard Rorty said that the novel was the 'characteristic genre of democracy', because of its role in widening the circle of sympathy people felt for others. Despite being a philosopher himself, he argued that fiction was a superior tool to reason when it came to bringing people together. A Christian and an atheist, for example, might not be able to reason their way to common sympathy, and may well get into a fight, because the very methods of reasoning they each relied on were parochial, born of the 'epistemic communities' of which they are a part. Only fiction has the power to cross the mental barricades, to make strangers intelligible to each other, because it moves people's hearts as well as engaging their minds.

Rorty gave the example of the 1852 novel *Uncle Tom's Cabin*, by Harriet Beecher Stowe, generally acknowledged to have had a profound effect on attitudes to slavery in America, due to its powerful portrayal of long-suffering Uncle Tom. The novel sold 300,000 copies in its first year of publication in America, and a million in Britain. It is said that when Abraham Lincoln met Stowe, as America's Civil War began, he remarked, 'So this is the little lady who started this great war.' (To me, this doesn't necessarily read as a compliment, though apparently it was one.)

Recently, scientists have become interested in exactly what it is about fiction that makes it so compelling. In 2011, Raymond Mar, a professor of psychology at York University in Canada, published a review of eighty-six fMRI brain scan studies and concluded that there was substantial overlap between the neural networks we use to understand stories and the ones we use to navigate our relationships. Novels offer us a kind of mental simulation of real life encounters, giving us useful practice in how to interpret the intentions, motives, longings and frustrations of friends, enemies, neighbours and lovers.[*] In 2013 researchers at the New School in New York found that people performed better on tests of social and emotional intelligence after reading fiction. Even more interestingly this applied to literary fiction, and not to plot-driven popular fiction. The reason, said the researchers, is that literary fiction leaves more to the imagination, encouraging readers to make more effort in interpreting the motives of characters. In the empathic realm as well as the epistemic one, mysteries stimulate more of our curiosity than puzzles.

The city acted as a multiplier of epistemic curiosity as well as empathic curiosity. Samuel Johnson saw that the bringing together of large numbers of people in one closely packed area generated an unprecedented intellectual ferment, telling Boswell: 'I will venture to say, there is more learning and science within the circumference of ten miles

---

[*] One of Mar's studies found a similar result in preschool-age children – the more stories they had read to them, the keener their ability to understand other minds. The effect was also produced by watching movies but not by watching television, an anomaly that Mar thinks may be explained by the fact that children often watch TV alone, but go to the movies with their parents, and thus are more likely to have conversations about *why* Alex the Lion wants to go back to the zoo. The empathic curiosity of children seems to be just as reliant on parents as epistemic curiosity is.

from where we now sit, than in all the rest of the world.' Together with the spread of books, this gave rise to the kind of accidental learning that came to be known as 'serendipity', a word coined by the aristocratic dilettante Horace Walpole. Writing to a friend in 1754, Walpole explained an unexpected discovery he had just made by reference to a Persian fairy tale, 'The Three Princes of Serendip'. The princes, he told his correspondent, were 'always making discoveries, by accident and sagacity, of things they were not in quest of . . . now do you understand serendipity?' The city was a serendipity generator.

For the first time, large numbers of adults were being permitted to live lives of intellectual curiosity and get paid for it. For most of human history, learning stopped the moment that maturity was reached and young adults could turn their attention to reproducing, feeding their family and fighting. It was only when scientific institutions and modern universities were formed, and the economic benefits of industrialisation and trade felt, that it became possible to excuse significant numbers of people from the duties of survival.

Even as curiosity's reputation has waxed and waned over the centuries, the distinction between epistemic and diversive curiosity has remained remarkably consistent. The eighteenth-century philosopher David Hume divided curiosity into two types: the 'love of knowledge', and the 'insatiable desire for knowing the actions and circumstances of... neighbours'. In the late nineteenth century, the American philosopher William James, brother of Henry, distinguished between curiosity that was 'scientific' and that generated by 'mere novelty'.

We are still enjoying the legacy of the Enlightenment's great cascade of curiosity; it inspired dozens of pivotal inventions, advanced our understanding of who we are and how we got here, and laid the foundations of modern political and legal arrangements. Today, more than ever, we need to harness the power of billions of enquiring minds if we are to overcome our global challenges. But curiosity is in peril again, this time for very different reasons than in the medieval era. The problem today is rooted in an abundance, rather than a scarcity, of information, and of ease rather than difficulty of access to it. We are in danger of losing our taste for intellectual exploration, just as curiosity ought to be entering its greatest moment since Franklin flew his kite.

The Age of Answers

Machines are for answers; humans are for questions.
                                                    Kevin Kelly

In 1945, Vannevar Bush, director of the United States Office of Scientific Research, published an essay in the *Atlantic* magazine, entitled 'How We May Think'. In it he expressed concern that the world's knowledge was growing too fast for anyone to keep up:

The difficulty seems to be, not so much that we publish unduly in view of the extent and variety of present day interests, but rather that publication has been extended far beyond our present ability to make real use of the record. The summation of human experience is being expanded at a prodigious rate, and the means we use for threading through the consequent maze to the momentarily important item is the same as was used in the days of square-rigged ships.

Bush acknowledged that great advances were being made in the compression of information, by way of microfilm technology; he foresaw a time in the not-too-distant future when the entire *Encyclopaedia Britannica* might be 'reduced to the volume of a matchbox'. But even given these advances, he worried that the cost and accessibility of such compression would be too high for most to participate in its benefits.

Access wasn't the only problem. Bush also argued that the way we store data, compressed or otherwise, was unfit for purpose. We filed it alphabetically and numerically. That meant we could trace a particular piece of information by following paths and sub-paths, as librarians did. But the more information there was, the more cumbersome such methods became. Furthermore, this method of organisation didn't reflect the working of the human mind, with its quicksilver ability to make unlikely connections between very different pieces of information.

Bush's hypothetical solution to these problems – at the time more of a fantasy than a concrete proposal – was a machine he called a 'memex' (a word he formed by combining 'memory' with 'index'). He imagined it as a desk, with a slanting translucent screen on top, together with a keyboard and 'a set of buttons and levers'. The user would be able to input all sorts of information to the memex on microfilm, along with his own notes, photographs and film reels.

The crucial operation of the memex was this: any item could be linked to any other. If the user was interested in, say, the history of the bow and arrow, he could, over time, construct an 'associative mesh' of data, from an encyclopaedia entry on medieval warfare, to an article on the Crusades, to a picture of a Turkish arrow. All of these items would be linked to each other, and, like neurons in the brain, each would have multiple connections. The user could choose to follow different 'trails' through the data; if he wanted to take a diversion from the history of warfare into the physics of elasticity, he could do so. Bush had anticipated the structure of the internet, which is built on association – on information about information – via the hyperlink. What he didn't foresee – apart from a machine that didn't require levers – was the astonishing increase in the speed with which information can be processed, or the extent to which it could be compressed.

Claude Shannon, who worked with Bush at Bell Laboratories, is now regarded as the father of modern information theory. In 1949 he drew up a table of the major stores of memory in the world. The biggest was the US Library of Congress, which could, at the time, be taken as a rough proxy for the sum total of recorded human knowledge. Shannon estimated that it contained one hundred trillion bits of information. Today, that amount of information can be stored on a disc drive that weighs a few pounds and costs less than a thousand dollars. As a consequence, information is everywhere, and everywhere it is multiplying: in government and business offices, in scientific laboratories, in homes and even in the streets.

The speed of this change has been breathtaking. In the vivid analogy of computer scientist Jaron Lanier, 'It's as if you kneel to plant the seed of a tree and it grows so fast that it swallows your whole town before you can even rise to your feet.' The planet is covered in a fast-growing jungle of information. Naturally, guides have emerged to help people find their own trails through it. Google has gone further towards its goal of organising the world's information than anyone could have predicted just ten years ago. And by harnessing the enthusiasm of volunteers and combining it with open source technology, Jimmy Wales, the founder of Wikipedia, has created an enterprise that represents a revolution in the relationship between humans and knowledge.*

---

* Wikipedia's critics complain about its unreliability. But surely unreliability is a price worth paying for astonishing comprehensiveness. It is best used in the way Wales suggests — as a first point of reference, never a last. In its messiness, argumentativeness and constant revisions, Wikipedia represents the way that science proceeds far better than the *Encyclopaedia Britannica*, with its august promise of fixed certainties, ever did. It reminds us that knowledge is *inherently* unreliable.

These online intermediaries between us and the world's information have their shortcomings and algorithmic biases. But the first thing to say about them is that they are indispensable, given the otherwise ungovernable amount of information now in circulation. The modern internet is now the best ever resource for the curious mind; from my laptop or mobile phone, I can instantly access essays on Bach cantatas or watch lectures on development economics and astrophysics from some of the finest minds in each field. I can pore over Shakespeare's first folio, scrutinise the brushstrokes on a Rembrandt, watch and rewatch the crucial scenes in *The Godfather*. I can sign up for courses at the world's great universities or join communities of people who are as interested in learning blues guitar as I am. I can scour the web for information that might be helpful to my business or spark a new idea for my book. Much or most of this I can do for free.

But despite this, we may be becoming a *less* curious society than eighteenth-century London. Curiosity is about the demand as well as the supply of information. It's about what we want, how we feel about it, and how much effort and time we are prepared to invest in it. It's also about discrimination; it involves choices about *which* knowledge we want to explore. As we've seen, the web can give us answers before we've even had time to think about the question. It can also make it too easy for us to ignore our own ignorance.

*

One day in 1945, a man named Percy Spencer was touring one of the laboratories he managed at Raytheon in Waltham, Massachusetts, a supplier of radar technology to the Allied forces fighting the Second World War. He was standing by a magnetron, a vacuum tube which generates microwaves to boost the sensitivity of radar, when he felt a strange sensation. Checking his pocket, he found his candy bar had melted. Curiosity aroused, he sent for a bag of popcorn, and held it up to the magnetron. The popcorn popped. Within a year, Raytheon made a patent application for a microwave oven.

The history of scientific discovery is peppered with breakthroughs that came about by accident, the most famous being Alexander Fleming's discovery of penicillin in 1928, prompted when Fleming noticed how a mould that floated into his Petri dish held the surrounding bacteria at bay. Spencer and Fleming didn't just get lucky. They were intensely curious people who had accumulated a vast knowledge of their field, and were engaged on quests of understanding and improvement. They were ready to spot and seize the significance of an anomaly when they came across one.

These days, we tend to associate serendipity with luck, and neglect what Horace Walpole called 'sagacity'. After he felt his candy bar melt, Spencer didn't shrug his shoulders and walk on, which is what most of us would probably have done. Only a man who knew as much about bacteria as Fleming, and who was as hungry to know more, would have clocked the significance of that stray spore. Louis Pasteur remarked that 'in the field of observation, chance favours only the prepared mind.' Curiosity prepares us for epiphanies by making us aware of our own blind spots, interested in our own ignorance. It makes us lucky.

The economist John Maynard Keynes once offered advice on how to conduct oneself in a bookshop:

A bookshop is not like a railway booking-office which one approaches knowing what one wants. One should enter it vaguely, almost in a dream, and allow what is there freely to attract and influence the eye. To walk the rounds of the bookshops, dipping in as curiosity dictates, should be an afternoon's entertainment.

This is very different to the advice you'd give someone on how to use Google, which, in Keynes's terms, is more like a railway booking-office – a place to visit when you know your destination. But a truly curious person knows that she doesn't always know what she wants to know about.

Discussing the future of his company, Google's co-founder Larry Page described the 'perfect search engine' as one that would 'understand exactly what I mean and give me back exactly what I want.' But what if I don't know what I want?

The question 'What do I *need* to learn?' isn't hard to answer; we're programmed with some of the answers by our DNA, and we know from birth that it's important to learn how to eat, or to decode and eventually reproduce those funny noises our parents make with their mouths. As we grow older there is no shortage of people – parents, teachers, bosses – telling us what we need to know in order to do well at school or at work. In this regard, the internet is unbeatable; when you know what you need to know, it can almost always help you find it. The question 'What do I *want* to learn?' is much more difficult. It's one of the most important questions of our lives, and the one question the internet can't help you with.

In the early days of the internet, its enthusiasts had a vision of it akin to Keynes's bookshop or Franklin's coffee house – a place in which users would enjoy random encounters and make unexpected connections. The term 'surfing' reflected this sense of free-ranging enquiry. Microsoft's slogan during the 1990s – 'Where do you want to go today?' – captured this sense of the online world as a space for endless adventure. As the writer Evegny Morozov has pointed out, the names of internet browsers – Explorer, Navigator, Safari – reflected a romantic idea of the web as a virgin territory, where everyone was free to explore their own individual interests, no matter how obscure or idiosyncratic.

Today, the internet is a precision-tooled, hyper-lubricated machine for the delivery of answers. Whatever you're looking for, whether it's information or entertainment, can be provided with awesome efficiency. Plug a question into Google and it will often come up with the answer without you needing to make another click. Hear a song when you're in a café, and you can purchase it there and then on your phone. Facebook encourages its users to stay safely within in its blue walls by providing them with everything they might want. Increasingly, we access internet services via mobile apps, which mean we don't even need to enter the web and risk its uncertainties. The Wild West has been settled, its ramshackle villages turned into air-conditioned malls.

The web is easier to search than ever, but because it meets our desires so efficiently, it doesn't necessarily stoke our curiosity. Curiosity is sustained by unanswered questions, and Google has all the answers; it never says 'I don't know'. In information terms, this has a tendency to make us all 'ignorant but happy', blithely unconcerned by what we don't yet know about.

Not everyone sees this as a problem. According to the technological evangelist Robert Scoble, 'The new world is you just open up Facebook and everything you care about will be streaming down the screen.' But being curious means wanting to find out about things you *don't* yet care about and *aren't* interested in – things you didn't know you were interested in until you find out that you are.

The media scholar Ethan Zuckerman of M.I.T. has noted that old-fashioned print media of the kind that emerged in the eighteenth century are – despite or rather because of their limitations – good at stimulating your curiosity by creating serendipity. A newspaper front page can draw your eye down from a story about Lady Gaga's dress towards one about a revolution in Tunisia. Good bookshops are still better than Amazon at attracting your attention to books you've never heard of before and didn't set out to acquire (a recent study found that people are twice as likely to buy a book on impulse in a bookstore than online). In this way, the old media were better at broadening our horizons. Google can answer anything you want, but it can't tell you what you ought to be asking.

When we widen our access to information, it doesn't follow that our curiosity widens too. Quite the opposite. James Evans, a sociologist at the University of Chicago, assembled a database of thity-four million scholarly articles published between 1945 and 2005. He analysed the citations included in the articles to see if patterns of research have changed as journals shifted from print to online. Given that it is much easier to search digital text than printed text, his working assumption was that he would find a much more diverse set of citations, as scholars used the web to broaden the scope of their research. Instead, he found that as journals moved online, scholars actually cited fewer articles than they had before. A broadening of available information had led to 'a narrowing of science and scholarship'.

Explaining his finding, Evans noted that search engines like Google tend to have a ratchet effect, making popular articles even more popular, thus quickly establishing and reinforcing a consensus about what's important and what isn't. Furthermore, the ease and efficiency of hyperlinks means that researchers bypassed many of the 'marginally related articles' print researchers would routinely stumble upon as they flipped the pages of a printed journal or book.

Online research was more efficient, predictable and tidy than library research, but precisely because of this it had the effect of shrinking the scope of investigation.

The web's ability to dissolve barriers of distance, culture and language has been much celebrated. But there is evidence that while the internet expands the horizons of those who want their horizons expanded, it encourages most of us to be more parochial. Ethan Zuckerman found that ninety-three per cent of the news consumed by American internet users is published in the United States. That actually makes it one of the *least* parochial nations; ninety-eight per cent of the traffic to news sites in France goes to domestic sites. 'Information may flow globally,' says Zuckerman, 'but our attention tends to be highly local and highly tribal.'

The economists Fernando Ferreira and Joel Waldfogel have studied the music-buying habits of consumers from twenty-two countries in the half century since 1960. You might expect that in the age of YouTube, iTunes and Spotify, our musical tastes would have become globalised and heterogeneous. But Ferreira and Waldfogel found that not only were consumers from all over the world biased towards music from their own country, but that this bias had *increased* since the turn of the century.

A serendipity deficit makes innovation harder, because innovation relies on unexpected collisions of knowledge and ideas. When everyone accesses the same information in the same way it becomes harder to make original connections. Zuckerman told me about a speech on serendipity that he gave to an audience of investment managers. At first he was nervous about holding their attention, but they hung on every word. 'In finance, everyone reads Bloomberg, so everyone sees the same information,' said Zuckerman. 'What they're looking for are strategies for finding inspiration from outside the information orbit.'*

It's not that the internet doesn't have the potential to open our minds to new information, other people and other worlds. It's that, all too often, this potential lies untapped. In the future, the people who are better at exploiting it will find themselves at an increasing advantage.

---

* For an excellent discussion of the internet and serendipity, read Zuckerman's 2013 book, *Rewire*.

CHAPTER 5

The Curiosity Dividend

Education is the single biggest factor in determining whether or not individuals are likely to prosper in today's world. The gap between the college-educated populations of developed countries and everyone else is growing wider. Most of us live in an economic environment that, more than ever before, rewards learners and penalises the ignorant or unskilled.

On a global scale, the nations with a higher proportion of young people at college are those whose economies tend to grow fastest. In Europe and in the US, the costs of higher education are rising at a greater rate than average incomes – but the cost of *not* being educated is rising even faster. In the US today, college graduates earn eighty per cent more than those who don't graduate from high school.

The gateway to higher education is academic performance at school. Naturally, then, an increasing amount of attention has been paid to the question of what makes some people do better at school than others. We know that socioeconomic factors play a big part, but what role is played by an individual's ability and outlook? The most exhaustively studied factor is intelligence. Although there continues to be controversy over the reliability and significance of IQ scores, there is plenty of evidence that intelligence, or 'cognitive ability', is strongly correlated with academic performance.

But IQ is far from the sole determinant of success. Every experienced teacher has stories about clever kids who left school without the qualifications that less talented peers achieved, and university tutors know that sometimes the most intelligent students are also the laziest. In recent years, psychologists studying differences in educational achievement have been paying more attention to the question of 'non-cognitive traits', by which they mean something like personality, or character. It's now recognised that the *attitude* students take towards the learning process, and the habits they practise, have a bigger impact on how well they do at school than previously accounted for. This effect becomes more pronounced at more advanced levels of education, as differences in intellectual capacity flatten out. A longitudinal study of elite British students found that personality traits account for *four times* as much variance in exam results than intelligence.

So which personality traits are important? The trait that has gained most attention from researchers is 'conscientiousness' and its related qualities: persistence, self-discipline, and what the psychologist Angela Duckworth termed 'grit' – the ability to deal with failure, overcome setbacks and focus on

long-term goals. This group of attitudes is consistently correlated with high achievement.* More recently, powerful
evidence has emerged of another personality trait with a
comparable impact on educational success.

Sophie von Stumm, a lecturer in psychology at Goldsmiths
University, led a review of existing research on individual
differences in academic performance, gathering data from
200 studies, covering a total of about 50,000 students. She
hypothesised that *intellectual curiosity* – the tendency to
'seek out, engage in, enjoy and pursue opportunities for
effortful cognitive activity' – would count towards success,
because students who possessed it would be hungry to learn
information and explore new ideas. The data proved her
right: von Stumm and her collaborators found that curiosity
had roughly as big an effect on performance as conscientiousness. When put together, the personality traits of
conscientiousness and curiosity count for as much as intelligence. A hungry mind, according to von Stumm, is the
'third pillar' of academic achievement.

In 2012, researchers at University College London carried
out a massive meta-analysis of studies published between
1997 and 2010, the product of 241 data sets, with the aim
of determining which aspects of a high school student's
background and personality best predict success at col-

---

* Conscientiousness is largely independent of intelligence, although there
is some evidence that less able individuals sometimes become more consci-
entious to compensate for lower levels of ability, while very intelligent individuals are tempted to 'coast'.

lege. Their findings are strikingly similar to von Stumm's. The researchers investigated three categories of potential predictors: demographic factors like sex and social class, conventional measures of cognitive ability like IQ and academic achievement in high school, and forty-two character traits which have at one time or another been held to be influential on educational outcomes, such as self-esteem or optimism. They found that demographic factors played little part in college success (factors like social class play their biggest role in determining who gets to college in the first place). The best predictors of success were intelligence and performance at school. After that, nothing else counted for much, except for conscientiousness and NFC – 'need for cognition', the scientific proxy for curiosity.

The logic is intuitive enough; an intelligent child won't reach her potential unless she applies consistent effort over time, and she is less likely to apply consistent effort if she is low on intrinsic desire to learn. But it's only now that researchers can quantify the importance of curiosity to educational outcomes. In fact, von Stumm thinks that curiosity may be the best single predictor of individual success, because it incorporates intelligence, persistence and hunger for novelty in one. People who are genuinely *interested* in what they're learning about tend to work harder at understanding it. We also know that the feeling of being interested enhances thinking. The psychologist Paul Silvia explains that when people are interested in what they're reading, they pay closer attention, process the information more efficiently, make more connections between new and existing knowledge, and attend to deeper questions raised by the text rather than just its surface features.

Whether or not we can raise the curiosity levels of our societies depends on several factors, including our education systems, child-rearing practices, teaching styles, and social attitudes. One of the things it depends on most is how we use the internet.

If Vannevar Bush, prophet of the world wide web, had been allowed to drop in on the twenty-first century he may have been simultaneously excited and disappointed. A user of the social news and discussion site Reddit recently posted the following question: 'If someone from the 1950s suddenly appeared today, what would be the most difficult thing to explain to them about today?' The most popular answer was this one:

> *I possess a device, in my pocket, that is capable of accessing the entirety of information known to man. I use it to look at pictures of cats and get into arguments with strangers.*

The term 'digital divide' emerged in the 1990s to describe the technology's haves and have-nots; those who could benefit from the educational benefits of the internet and those excluded from them. It inspired efforts to spread access as widely as possible, particularly to low-income families, and, partly as a result, the divide has narrowed. But increased access to the internet isn't, in itself, a social good; what matters is how it is used. As Danah Boyd, a senior researcher at Microsoft, puts it, the spread of internet access 'mirrors and magnifies existing problems we've been ignoring'. Foremost among them is that not everyone is interested in exercising their epistemic curiosity.

The Kaiser Foundation, a US think-tank, has been surveying the media habits of Americans for over a decade, and it has found that American children now spend at least ten hours a day with digital devices, an increase of over fifty per cent since 1999. The poorer a household is, the more time its children spend glued to a device; according to the Kaiser study, children and teenagers whose parents do not have a college degree spent ninety minutes more per day exposed to media than children from higher socioeconomic families. This divide is widening; in 1999, the difference was just sixteen minutes. It turns out that when most people get their hands on a computer, rather than pursue their curiosity what they want to do is play Angry Birds. 'Despite the educational potential of computers, the reality is that their use for education . . . is minuscule compared to their use for pure entertainment,' said Vicky Rideout, author of the study. 'Instead of closing the achievement gap, they're widening the time-wasting gap.'

Another US study, this one a survey of teachers carried out by Pew Research, found that ninety per cent of teachers agreed that digital technologies were creating 'an easily distracted generation with short attention spans'. Three out of four teachers surveyed said that they believed students had been conditioned by the internet to find quick answers. In interviews with researchers from Common Sense Media, teachers described the 'Wikipedia problem' – students are so used to finding answers within a few clicks that they balk at the hard work of investigating problems which don't yield answers quickly. As one high school teacher said of her pupils: 'They need skills that are different than 'Spit, spit, there's the answer.'

The only sensible answer to the question, 'Is the internet making us stupid or more intelligent?' is 'Yes'. The internet presents us with more opportunities to learn than ever before, and also allows us not to bother. It is a boon to those with a desire to deepen their understanding of the world, and also to those who are only too glad not to have to make the effort. If you want to watch the black-spotted puffer fish in its natural habitat, examine a Gutenberg Bible or discover who invented the paper clip, then you can do so on the web. Similarly, if you want to take courses in French, or art history, or share your epistemic enthusiasms, however obscure, with communities of people who are interested in the same things, you can.

But if you're incurious – or, like most of us, a little lazy – then will you use the internet to look at pictures of cats and get into arguments with strangers. You will use it to get quick answers to questions that you might otherwise have to take your time over, think harder on and absorb more deeply as a result. The internet will effectively take over the functions normally performed by your instinct for enquiry. Your curiosity will be outsourced, and before you know it, you will forget how to practise it.

Rather than a great dumbing-down, it's likely that we are at the beginning of a cognitive polarisation – a division into the curious and the incurious. People who are inclined to set off on intellectual adventures will have more opportunities to do so than ever in human history; people who merely seek quick answers to someone else's questions will fall out of the habit of asking their own, or never learn it in the first place. In the blunt formulation of the writer Kevin Drum, 'The internet is making smart people smarter and dumb people dumber.'

As this cognitive divide develops, it will feed into and exacerbate existing socioeconomic inequality, via the education system. Parental discipline and good teachers will help get pupils through high school and into college, but their progress will be supercharged by an intrinsic desire to learn. Our education systems appear to be failing to inculcate this desire, particularly at the higher level. In the US, the Wabash National Study tracks the progress of 2,200 students during their four years at college. The students complete an array of surveys and tests at three points – when they first arrive on campus, at the end of their first year, and at the end of their fourth year. The survey's most striking finding is that academic motivation declines steeply over the first year at college – and never recovers.

At the same time, US colleges are demanding less of their students than they used to. Perhaps as a result, students are getting lazier. In 1961, students spent an average of twenty-four hours a week studying. Today's students spend a little more than half that time. The educationalists Richard Keeling and Richard Hersh argue that colleges and universities increasingly see themselves passively, as 'a kind of bank with intellectual assets that are available to students'. It's a state of affairs that will only worsen the curiosity divide, because it means that curious students will succeed disproportionately versus the incurious.

Traditional universities are increasingly vulnerable to competition from online providers of education, like Coursera and the Khan Academy. Established institutions like Harvard and Yale are also offering MOOCs (massive open online courses). For students who know what they want, MOOCs provide an attractive low-cost option. But to get the most out of a MOOC, even more so than at a bricks-and-mortar university, you need to be a good self-motivator – and the best motivator of learning is epistemic curiosity. Without the incentive of wanting to get the most out of a big financial investment, or the daily encouragement of real-life meetings with students and teachers, the MOOC student is thrown back on her inner desire to learn. Unless it is unusually high, she may find it hard to stay the course. According to the *New York Times*, 'less than 10 per cent of MOOC students finish the courses they sign up for on their own.'

We live in a world in which the competition for jobs is getting fiercer than ever as the global labour force expands, while smart machines take over more of the tasks that were once the exclusive province of humans. Meanwhile, the internet extends the opportunity to learn to people who previously didn't have it. The combination of these factors will reward curiosity and penalise incuriosity on a global scale, because curiosity is such a great motivator to learn. Here's an extract from an interview with the economist Tyler Cowen about his 2013 book, *Average Is Over*:

> *The more information that's out there, the greater the returns to just being willing to sit down and apply yourself ... So if you're an individual, say from China or India, and you're really smart and motivated, you're going to do much better in this new world than say 10 or 20 years ago. But there are a lot of people in the wealthier countries, I wouldn't describe them as lazy, but they're not super motivated. They think they can more or less get by. I think in relative terms those people are already starting to see lower wages because they're not quite the prize commodities they think they are.*

John Dewey, the American philosopher and educationalist, writing in 1910, proposed three stages of curiosity. The first is the child's hunger to explore and probe its surroundings – it is instinctual rather than intellectual. In the second, curiosity becomes more social, as children realise that other people are useful sources of information about the world, and begin asking an endless series of 'why' questions; the specific questions themselves aren't as important as the habit of gathering and assimilating information. In the third stage, curiosity is 'transformed into interest in problems provoked by the observation of things and the accumulation of material'. In this final stage, curiosity becomes a force that deepens the bond between the individual and the world, adding layers of interest, complexity and delight to her experience.

John Dewey didn't think everyone would reach this third stage. He regarded curiosity as a fragile quality, which required a constant effort to maintain:

> In a few people, intellectual curiosity is so insatiable that nothing will discourage it, but in most its edge is easily dulled and blunted . . . Some lose it in indifference or carelessness; others in a frivolous flippancy; many escape those evils only to become incased in a hard dogmatism which is equally fatal to the spirit of wonder.

It is easy to blame the internet for making us stupid. But the only person or thing that can make you stupid, or incurious, is you. Those who are tempted to use the web as a way of avoiding intellectual effort may forget how to be curious at all. Those who use it as a springboard to sustained intellectual explorations are likely to achieve more at school and university and to reap increasingly higher rewards at work. The future belongs to those who choose curiosity.

CHAPTER 6

The Power of Questions

Questions are places in your mind where answers fit. If you haven't asked the question, the answer has nowhere to go.

Clay Christensen

In 1990 Dan Rothstein was working as a community organiser in Lawrence, an old mill town in Massachusetts. The town's prosperity had been built on a thriving textile industry, long since departed. It was now a town with high unemployment, high crime rates and thousands of poor families dependent on public services for survival. Rothstein was in charge of a dropout prevention program; he worked with families whose children weren't attending school, to try and keep them in the system. He knew that if they fell through the cracks at this age they would probably never recover their futures.

Most of the parents with whom Rothstein worked were

loving, well meaning and keen for their children to do well. But they were desperately overstretched. Many were single parents working two or more jobs. Often, English was their second language (the town had a high Latino population), which complicated the parents' efforts to communicate with their children's teachers or with social services. Rothstein soon discovered that their difficulties went deeper than linguistic capability, however. Something was preventing them from speaking up. 'They would go along to the school to see the headmaster or the other teachers. They would sit through a lecture about their son or daughter's attendance record. And then they would come home, feeling as powerless as they were before.'

After hearing many of these stories, Rothstein zeroed in on the real problem. It wasn't that the parents didn't know what to ask. It was that they didn't know *how* to ask. They didn't have the skill, taken for granted by middle-class people, of using questions to extract information or elicit help from officials.

Rothstein and his colleagues set out to help. They started by creating lists of questions that the parents could use. But they soon found that it was hard to come up with the right pre-written questions for every situation that arose. In some cases they only were compounding the problem, because the parents were becoming increasingly dependent on their help.

It became evident that it wasn't enough just to suggest questions; Rothstein and his fellow organisers would have to train people in the art of asking them. 'Question-asking,' Rothstein told me, 'is a sophisticated skill. People learn it in middle-class households and then in elite professional fields like the law or education.' We're not conscious of learning it; very few of us have taken classes in 'how to construct a question' or received lectures on it from our parents. But we learn it via osmosis from those around us.

Rothstein put together a few simple principles of question-asking, like how to ask a closed question or an open question – one that can be answered 'yes' or 'no' versus one that induces a longer conversation with the interlocutor. He found that the parents he worked with picked them up quickly and started to put them to work, with encouraging results.

Rothstein realised that the teaching of question-asking had the potential to change lives. It could help families in many different situations: at parent-teacher meetings, at the unemployment bureau, when dealing with the police or with commercial services. The more he thought about it, the more important a skill it seemed. Question-asking, he came to believe, is fundamental to being human. 'You know, it's almost a physical feeling, isn't it?' he said to me. 'When you walk away from an encounter and think, *I wish I'd asked that.*'

But while we're all born with the capacity to ask questions, our ability to do so is unequally distributed.

In 1930, a psychologist called Dorothea McCarthy observed a hundred and forty children in Minneapolis, aged between eighteen and fifty-four months. She recorded the first fifty utterances of each child as the child talked to a researcher. She found that upper-class children asked more questions than lower-class children. This class difference was evident remarkably early – from the age of two years old.

A similar pattern emerged in a 1984 study by the British researchers Barbara Tizard and Martin Hughes, who recorded four-year-old girls talking to their mothers at home. The proportion of conversations that turned on questions asked by the child were greater in middle-class homes than working-class ones. Middle-class children were especially likely to ask curiosity-based questions: 'how' and 'why' questions. They were also more likely to engage their mother in what the authors of the study termed 'passages of intellectual search' – a series of linked questions, each following on from the other.

Tizard and Hughes reported conversations in which middle-class children applied their own brand of rigour to the answers proffered by parents. Four-year-old Rosy engaged her mother in a long exchange about why a window cleaner was given money. Her mother responded, 'Well, the window cleaner needs money, doesn't he?' 'Why?' asked Rosy, unsatisfied. 'To buy clothes for his children and food for them to eat.' Rosy pointed out, quite reasonably, 'Sometimes window cleaners don't have children.' Such exchanges aren't unique to today's less deferential mores. The scientist and educationalist Nathan Isaacs, writing in 1930, recalls a girl of nearly four asking her mother, 'Why don't we milk pigs?' Her mother's reply — 'Because they have little ones of their own to feed' — didn't satisfy her. 'So do cows have calves,' she pointed out. As Tizard and Hughes drily remark, young children are capable of pursuing knowledge with 'penetrating, remorseless logic'.

Why are middle-class children more likely to use questions to explore their curiosity? Not necessarily because they are getting more answers. Tizard and Hughes found that working-class mothers were just as likely to answer their child's questions. Rather, it was because they were getting more questions. Mothers who asked more questions of their children had children who asked more questions of them. Question-asking, it turned out, is contagious.

An American study in 1992 provided more evidence for this finding. The researchers studied parent-child interactions in the homes of forty children. They found a very wide variance between different families in the number of questions that parents asked of their kids. The tendency to ask many questions went along with a conversational style in which parents would take up, expand and discuss what their children had said. The parents who asked fewer questions were more likely to issue prohibitions: 'Stop', 'Don't do that.' Children who observed their parents using language as a tool for cognitive exploration, rather than just control, were more likely to emulate that usage.

Just as some households are more curious than others, so are some cultures. A 2011 study recorded the everyday conversations of three- and five-year olds living in villages or small towns on four different continents: Belize, Kenya, Nepal and Samoa. The children were from poor families, their parents subsistence farmers or low-wage labourers. Information-seeking questions made up about one-tenth of their remarks – a similar proportion to that observed among American kids. But whereas one quarter of the American children's information-seeking questions started with 'how' or 'why', such exploratory questions were very rare in the non-Western communities. In fact, they accounted for just one in twenty.

One of the authors of the study, the anthropologist Robert Munroe, noted that mothers in these communities tended to place a strong emphasis on their children being obedient and respectful. They rarely hesitated to scold or beat their children if they deemed them to have spoken or acted out of line. Dialogue with children seemed to be conceived of in almost exclusively functional terms, as a means of instruction and organisation rather than as an exchange of information, ideas or jokes. Across the four countries, it was children in Samoa who asked the greatest proportion of information-seeking questions, and the children in Kenya who asked the least.

Paul Harris speculates that this is because of the respective levels of education in those countries. The Samoan parents were more likely to have attended school when they were young and thus to have grown up with a model of conversation as a way of exchanging information. 'When they eventually become parents, they are likely to reactivate that model and use it as a guide in raising their own children.' The study also suggests that open-ended, intellectually inviting questions are what you have time for after you're done with the business of survival. If middle-class families in affluent economies are more curious it's partly because they can afford to be; their basic needs for food, warmth and security are taken care of and they can devote cognitive resources to curiosity.

As we've seen, using language as a tool to satisfy and further one's curiosity is a habit that middle-class children are more likely to learn than poor and working-class children. This isn't just a shame in terms of the intellectual development of poor children; it perpetuates and exacerbates the social disadvantage they started out with.

Annette Lareau is a sociologist at the University of California who has, over the past twenty years, done more than anyone else to document the differences between growing up in a poor or working-class household in the United States versus growing up in a middle-class household. Her work — itself a testament to the power of curiosity — gets beneath the hard facts and figures of inequality to the lived reality of social class.

At the heart of Lareau's research is close, almost novelistic observation. She or one of her team spends weeks virtually living with the families they are studying. They gather information by talking to the children and their parents about their daily routines, hopes and fears. But what they really do is observe. They are there in the mornings when the family is getting ready for the day ahead. They are there when the children get home from school. They are there at meal times and during TV sessions. They accompany family members on sports days, school visits and trips to the doctor, and they witness rows, tears, hugs, conversations, games and chores.

The researchers make notes on everything they witness, and after they have completed their time with a family, Lareau turns their observations and reflections into a written narrative that describes the texture of that family's daily life. At the same time, she brings her deep experience and sharp analytical mind to bear on the material, identifying the social dynamics of each family's life, looking for significant similarities and differences in the way families interact with the world around them.

Based on this close-up work, Lareau has concluded that working-class families and middle-class families tend to pursue two very different methods of child-rearing, and that these contribute in subtle but powerful ways to the perpetuation of inequality. Middle-class parents are more likely to pursue a policy of *concerted cultivation*. They think of their child as someone whose talents must be assiduously nurtured, and devote a lot of resources to doing so. They organise the life of the family around their children's needs, providing an activity-packed hothousing that is designed to develop their child's abilities to the maximum extent.

Take the Williams family, with whom Lareau spent time while putting together the material that formed the basis of her influential book, *Unequal Childhoods*. The Williams family lived in an expensively furnished home in what Lareau called 'a major north-eastern city'. Alexander Williams, nine years old at the time of the study, was the happy, bright and lively child of Mr and Mrs Williams, both professionals with university educations. In a typical week, Alexander attended a piano lesson, choir practice, Sunday school, church choir, baseball and soccer practice and games. His parents read to him when he was younger and now encourage his own reading. They helped him with his schoolwork, engaged him in intellectually challenging conversations across the dinner table and constantly elicited his thoughts, opinions and feelings. The Williams parents both had demanding jobs, but their main project was their child.

Working-class families are more likely to pursue what Lareau calls a *natural growth* style of parenting. While no less loving than middle-class parents, working-class parents spend less time, effort and expense developing their children's talents, and involve them in fewer organised activities. This isn't necessarily through choice; poorer parents have to focus on getting through the month, and are lucky if they have any money, time or energy left over for piano lessons and reading sessions. The children of working-class households are likely to spend more time entertaining themselves on their own.

Lareau doesn't approve or disapprove of one parenting style over another. The kids raised in 'natural growth' households were often happy, and lived lives according with some of our fondest ideals of childhood; they enjoyed long hours doing little but daydreaming or playing their own games, alone or with friends. The middle-class children in her study were more easily frustrated when they were given nothing to do, and their sense of entitlement could manifest itself in unappealing ways.

But, says Lareau, there's no doubt that concerted cultivation better prepares children for the demands that modern society will make of them as adults. Modern workplaces and institutions – even education institutions – place a premium on assertive, confident individuals in command of powerful linguistic and reasoning abilities. One of the primary skills that a child raised under concerted cultivation learns is how to come up with their own questions.

When Mrs Williams took Alexander on a routine visit to the doctor, Lareau joined them. During the drive, Mrs Williams spoke to her son: 'Alexander, you should be thinking of questions you might want to ask the doctor. You can ask him anything you want. Don't be shy. You can ask anything.' Alex considered this, then said, 'I have some bumps under my arms from my deodorant.' 'Really?' said his mother, 'Well, you should ask the doctor.' In the examination room, the doctor began going through what he called 'the routine questions'. As he did so he noted that Alex was 'in the ninety-fifth percentile' in height. Alex interrupted him:

ALEX: I'm in the what?

DOCTOR: It means that you're taller than more than ninety-five out of a hundred young men when they're, uh, ten years old.

ALEX: I'm not ten.

DOCTOR: Well, they graphed you at ten. You're – nine years and ten months. They usually take the closest year to get that graph.

Lareau doesn't suggest that Alex was being rude in this exchange or during the rest of his visit. But by interrupting an authority figure with his own question he was displaying the kind of confidence and presumption of self-importance that only a child from a middle-class household is likely to possess.

Middle-class children use their superior language skills to 'customise' whatever situation they are in, says Lareau. Later in life, this serves them well, as they make their way through the education system and then the world of work. Adults from middle-class households are adept at maximising the opportunities that come their way, which are themselves more likely to be abundant than for a child from a working-class family. They are skilled at bending situations and structures to their own will. Adults from working-class families are more likely to be like the adults that Dan Rothstein worked with in Massachusetts – unable to impose themselves on the often anonymous and uncaring face of institutions vital to their well-being.

In another vignette from the life of the Williams family, Alex and his mother are discussing his homework project at the kitchen table, as his father washes the dishes. When his father jokingly suggests that he should copy some answers from a book, Alex, calling his bluff, threatens to take him up on the idea.

When his father hastily demurs, Alex's mother says to Alex, 'There's a word for that you know, plagiarism.' Alex makes it clear that he already knows the word, and introduces the concept of copyright to the conversation. The family then begin arguing over definitions ('They all begin talking at once.'). This kind of conversation – routine in many middle-class families – instils curiosity and the linguistic confidence to pursue it.

It's certainly not that working-class children are inherently less curious. Indeed, as Lareau remarked in an email to me, working class children can be said to have *more* opportunity to express genuine curiosity, because they're not as hothoused and hyper-scheduled as middle-class children, and are thus allowed more time to follow their own whims. When they do land upon something they love doing, Lareau told me, they are more likely to be in control of it: 'In the rare cases when the working-class children did enrol in an organised activity, the children were the ones driving the process, with more heartfelt interest and enthusiasm than the children in middle-class families.'*

* This may help to explain why pupils who have thrived at schools which provide a hothousing, activity-packed environment sometimes find it hard

But middle-class families are better at instilling the habit of question-asking into their children. They are constantly quizzing them, and making themselves available to be quizzed. By doing so, says Lareau, they are 'training their children to be curious'.

Even if we were raised to ask questions, we can easily fall out of the habit as adults, or neglect to do so at crucial moments. In his book *Will Your Next Mistake Be Fatal?* the business professor Robert Mittelstaedt argues that a failure to ask questions is often the root cause of disasters. He cites the most famous disaster of all – the sinking of the *Titanic*. Once its maiden voyage was under way, reports of icebergs came in from nearby ships: '*Titanic* received many incoming messages warning of ice, but there is no mention of her enquiring of others for updates or more information. What if someone was curious enough to ask for more information from the ships in the area?' Afterwards, several planners

---

to progress after leaving. The KIPP schools, which serve children from underprivileged American neighbourhoods, have a deservedly stellar reputation for getting children who otherwise would have been unlikely to complete their schooling to qualify for college. Their strategy involves taking up as much of the children's time as possible, with longer school hours, shorter breaks, out-of-school activities and pastoral care, and packed schedules. Once KIPP students get to university, however, they have a higher-than-average dropout rate. This are several possible reasons for this, but one of them might be that success at university requires a higher degree of self-motivation than at high school, especially one which (with the best of intentions and excellent results) is constantly directing its pupils' attention.

and shipbuilders involved admitted to having had questions about the ship's safety that they didn't raise in front of colleagues, for fear of appearing foolish.

Questions weaponise curiosity, turning it into a tool for changing behaviours. Michael Marquardt, author of *Leading with Questions*, quotes the former CEO of Dow Chemical, Mike Parker: 'A lot of bad leadership comes from an inability or unwillingness to ask questions. I have watched talented people – people with much higher IQs than mine – who have failed as leaders. They can talk brilliantly, with a great breadth of knowledge, but they're not very good at asking questions. So while they know a lot at a high level, they don't know what's going on way down in the system. Sometimes they are afraid of asking questions, but what they don't realise is that the dumbest questions can be very powerful. They can unlock a conversation.'*

In February 2002, the US Defence Secretary Donald Rumsfeld held a press conference to discuss the intense pressure that America was exerting on Saddam Hussein's

---

* Of course, not all questions are designed to elicit information. Often, even without realising we're doing it, we use questions as a disguise for statements we don't wish to make outright, like *'You're incompetent'* – questions that are meant to prove how clever we are, or how stupid someone else is. Roger Schwarz, an organisational psychologist and leadership consultant, reminds us that 'It's not enough to ask questions. You have to be genuinely curious.' He advises his clients to adopt the 'you idiot' test. It works like this: mentally recite to yourself the question you're about to ask. At the end of your private question, add the words, 'you idiot'. If the question still sounds natural, don't ask it.

regime. Rumsfeld was asked whether there was any substantial evidence linking the government of Iraq with the supply of weapons of mass destruction to terrorist groups. His reply included a complex formulation that would become inextricably associated with him: 'There are known knowns; there are things we know that we know. There are known unknowns; that is to say there are things that, we now know we don't know. But there are also unknown unknowns — there are things we do not know, we don't know.'

At the time, the statement was derided as the product of a confused mind. But despite what most people regard as the failure of Rumsfeld's project in Iraq, it has since been re-evaluated. The linguist Geoffrey Pullum describes the statement as 'impeccable syntactically, semantically, logically and rhetorically.' Rumsfeld was talking about the limits of US intelligence, but he was also suggesting how to think about the gaps in our knowledge.

The catastrophic problems encountered and created by the American occupiers of Iraq are well documented. The Bush administration severely underestimated the number of troops that would be required to keep order across the country, and overestimated the likelihood that Iraq's institutions would keep functioning in the aftermath of war. The journalist James Fallows, in an exhaustively researched article for the *Atlantic*, showed that it wasn't that the Bush administration hadn't been warned about such problems, but rather that it wilfully ignored the warnings, even when they came from within the administration.

The US State Department, which had seasoned Iraq and Middle East experts on its staff, produced long reports which presciently identified the challenges that America would face after invasion: the retreat of Saddam's army into a guerrilla campaign, the ruination of Iraq's infrastructure, the fact that the only people who knew how to keep the country running were also members of Saddam's ruling party. But these reports, and the people who authored them, were disregarded. Bush, Rumsfeld and Cheney had a plan, they were determined to stick to it, and that made them resolutely incurious about anything that might throw that plan into question. They didn't ask the right questions because they didn't want to know about their own information gaps. Rumsfeld's call to consider 'unknown unknowns' wasn't absurd — it was smart. The tragedy is that he didn't follow his own advice.

It's frequently observed that as small companies grow into large corporations their creativity and dynamism tends to decline, along with their awareness of the world they operate in. They make poor decisions based on patchy information, and get stuck with misconceptions about their competitors and consumers. Their field of vision narrows to a tunnel. One reason for this is that in bureaucracies there is often an incentive for senior managers to stop asking questions. Sir Francis Bacon's famous maxim is turned on its head — ignorance becomes power.

In October 2010, Jerome Keviel, a former trader at the

European bank Société Générale, was sentenced to five years in prison. Two years before, he had carried out a series of trades that had resulted in losses of nearly $7 billion for his employer. Ever since the story broke, senior bosses at Société Générale had claimed that Keviel had been operating entirely under the radar – that they had no knowledge of his actions, and certainly hadn't authorised them. Keviel insisted all along that his managers knew what was going on but turned a blind eye as long as he kept making profits. His managers denied this, and it was impossible to prove otherwise. Similar disputes arose during the scandals that shook News International in 2011 and 2012. Senior managers, starting with James and Rupert Murdoch, were keen to show that they had no knowledge of what their employees were up to, even at the risk of sounding as if they were embarrassingly out of touch with what was happening in their organisations. At SocGen and News International, *knowing what not to know* was itself indispensable knowledge.

Linsey McGoey, a sociologist at the University of Essex, studies 'strategic ignorance' – the circumstances in which cultivating ignorance becomes more advantageous than cultivating knowledge. Ignorance, as a deliberate choice, can be used to reinforce prejudice and discrimination. McGoey cites the example of a ruling by the US Justice Department in 1986, at the height of the Aids panic, which stated that employers could fire individuals with Aids as long as they could claim to be ignorant of the established medical fact that Aids did not pose a danger in the workplace.

A policy of deliberate ignorance is often adopted by those who wish to protect their own power. Large organisations are particularly prone to it because they have layers of managers whose priority is not innovation or improved effectiveness, but the retention of their positions. As McGoey points out, strategic ignorance played an important role in the financial crisis of 2008; it wasn't that bankers didn't see the warning signs of catastrophe so much as they *chose* not to see them. The boards of the banks that succumbed to the financial crisis of 2008 were stuffed with seasoned executives who knew a little about the highly risky activities of parts of the company for which they were nominally responsible, but decided not to look too closely at them in case doing so put their power, and their bonuses, at risk.

Success can breed deliberate ignorance. It seems to be a law of business that the more a firm grows, the less it values difficult questions. Why question what (apparently) works? In his classic book on innovation, *The Innovator's Dilemma*, Clayton Christensen showed how even the smartest of companies can fail because they stop asking how they can do things better. Precisely because they have become so successful at catering to customers who buy their most profitable products or services, market-leading companies often neglect what is happening at the unglamorous low end of the market. Smaller competitors, providing cheaper alternatives, are driven by necessity to ask fresh questions about the changing needs of customers. That makes them more innovative, and the cheap but effective products they create can disrupt and eventually overturn the dominance of the larger company. Questions are the best weapons of the weak against the strong, but only because the strong unilaterally disarm.

Michael Marquardt identifies four reasons that we don't ask questions when we ought to. First, because of a desire to protect ourselves from the danger of looking stupid. How many times have you been part of a conversation and had a question nagging away at you but been too scared to ask it in case everyone in the room laughs at you? And then found out that it *was* a good question, because someone else asks it, to approving murmurs – or even worse, because it goes unasked and unanswered and later explodes into a problem that could have been avoided.

Second, because we're too busy. Good questions require time to germinate and grow. When we're over-occupied with things to do we focus on action at the expense of thinking and questioning. Third, because the culture discourages questioning. In authoritarian countries, questions that spring from genuine curiosity are discouraged. In organisations that suffer from some form of what Irving Janis termed 'groupthink', people who ask awkward questions can quickly be made to feel unwelcome. Even in cultures that value different opinions, a subtler interdiction can operate; the social trends expert Daniel Yankelovich observed that American culture 'rushes to action'. Often, he says, the only question that gets a hearing is, 'What are we going to *do* about it?' The fourth reason we don't ask questions, says Marquardt, is that we lack the skills required to ask them.

Asking good questions stimulates the hunger to know more by opening up exciting new known unknowns. A sixth-grade student in California remarked to Dan Rothstein, 'Just when you think you know all that you need to know, you ask another question and discover how much more there is to learn.'

CHAPTER 7

The Importance of Knowing

For knowledge to the understanding is as acceptable as light to the eyes; and children are pleased and delighted with it exceedingly, especially if they see that their enquiries are regarded, and that their desire of knowing is couraged and commended.

John Locke

At last gleams of light have come . . .

Charles Darwin

In 1999, Sugata Mitra was teaching computer programming to middle-class professionals at a college in New Delhi. Next to the building where he worked was a slum, which his office overlooked. Gazing out of his window, Mitra would occasionally wonder if the children in those overcrowded shacks would ever have the chance to use a computer – and if so, what they might do with it.

CURIOUS

After class, Mitra's affluent students would share stories about their children, boasting of their high-achieving sons and daughters doing amazing things with expensive computers. Mitra was suitably impressed. But one day, a question dropped into his head and refused to leave: 'How come it's just the rich people who have these gifted children?'

The question spurred an impromptu experiment. Mitra made a hole in the boundary wall of the slum, and fixed an internet-connected computer monitor and keyboard in it, three feet off the ground. Children from the slum gathered around, eyes wide. 'What is this?' they asked. Mitra shrugged, pretended ignorance, and walked away.

About eight hours later, Mitra returned to the same spot. He found the children gathered around the computer, browsing the internet. Mitra was dumbfounded. He knew that these children had never touched or even seen a computer before. How had they become competent users of the internet within hours of getting their hands on one? When he told his colleagues, one of them proposed a simple explanation – a teacher must have been passing by and stopped to show the children how to use the mouse. Mitra was sceptical but conceded it was possible. He repeated the experiment in a village, three hundred miles from Delhi, deep in rural India, 'where the chances of a passing software engineer are very low.'

When Mitra returned to the village two months after installing the computer he found children happily playing games on it. 'We want a faster processor,' they told him. 'And a better mouse.' When Mitra asked them about how they had learned to use the computer they explained, in tones of mild irritation, that since he had given them a machine that worked only in English, they first had had to teach themselves English in order to use it.

Mitra repeated his experiment several times in different parts of the Indian countryside, getting the same results everywhere. Video he took of children playing with one of his hole-in-the-wall computers shows them teaching each other; friends teaching friends, younger brothers teaching elder sisters. Mitra began publishing his findings in a series of papers. He summarised his experiments like this: 'In nine months a group of children left alone with a computer in any language will reach the same standard as an office secretary in the West.' He knew this because he had seen it happen over and over again.

Mitra now asked an even more ambitious question of his research. Could Tamil-speaking children in a south Indian village learn something that required a really sophisticated level of understanding, in English, from a street-side computer? Mitra suspected that the answer was no, and hoped that this experiment would at least make the case for more teachers. He chose a village and installed computers, on to which he downloaded material on DNA replication, and left the village's children to it. Two months later, he returned to set the children a test. They flunked it. On a visit two months after that, the children told him they had still made no progress. Mitra wasn't surprised. Then a little girl raised her hand and explained, in broken Tamil and English, 'Apart from the fact that improper replication of the DNA molecule causes disease, we haven't understood anything.'

Mitra realised that the children had made progress even if they weren't aware of doing so, and even if they were still achieving low scores on his test. He decided that they needed an adult supervisor. He asked a young woman, an accountant who spent a lot of time in the village and knew its children, to help him. She told Mitra that she didn't know anything about DNA replication. Mitra advised her to use 'the grandmother method' – stand behind them as they play on the computer, make encouraging noises, and ask them what they're doing.

Two months later, their scores had jumped to fifty per cent on his test. The children of this poor village in Tamil Nadu had caught up with the children Mitra was using as an experimental control – pupils of a wealthy private school in New Delhi, whose parents were the kind of people to whom Mitra taught computer programming.

Mitra, now a Professor of Educational Technology at Newcastle University, believes that the children of southern India have a message for us in the West: it's time to change the way we learn. Our education systems, he says, are designed to meet a challenge that no longer exists. Our schools are good at producing efficient administrators capable of running an empire, but less good at cultivating curious learners. The internet has made teachers – in the sense of adult transmitters of knowledge – unnecessary.

All learning can be approached in the same way those children in Tamil Nadu met the challenge of learning about DNA replication — with a broadband connection and a little help from their friends.

Mitra's research became widely known about after he gave a TED talk (from which my account is adapted).* He closes his talk by suggesting that the arrival of the internet demands a radical new conception of human cognition, first articulated by the technology visionary Nicholas Negroponte. The internet's infinite storage capacity means that we no longer need to keep facts and information in our own brains. Instead of memorising knowledge, we are free to explore it. In Negroponte's formulation, 'knowing is obsolete'.

A school is a crucible of curiosity. It can imbue the fledgling desire to learn of young children with strength and sinew, or it can it be the place where it is allowed to atrophy. If you're concerned about the role of curiosity in society, as I am, then you have a stake in the perennial debate over what schools are *for*. The fault line in these debates is this — should schools be places where adults transmit to children the academic knowledge that society deems valuable?

---

* TED, which stands for Technology, Entertainment and Design, started off as an annual conference of ideas in California and has since become a global brand which champions 'ideas worth spreading'. In 2013, TED awarded Mitra a $1 million prize to pursue further experiments in 'self-organized learning'.

Or places where children are allowed to follow their own curiosity, wherever it takes them?

Professor Mitra's vision of technology-enabled education reform is best seen in the context of this long-running dispute. The proposition 'knowing is obsolete' sounds excitingly futuristic, but its roots extend back through centuries. The idea of what is sometimes called a 'curiosity-driven' education – an education largely free of the necessity to memorise academic knowledge imparted by adults – is so attractive that we reinvent it every generation.

Mitra doesn't mention any intellectual influences, but it's possible to trace his major arguments and presumptions back to one of the founders of the late eighteenth-century cultural movement that became known as Romanticism. In *Émile (or On Education)*, published in 1762, Jean-Jacques Rousseau used the fictional example of a boy called Émile to argue that a child can learn everything he needs to without interference from adults. A child's natural curiosity is the only teacher he requires. 'Let us . . . omit from our early studies such knowledge as had no natural attraction for us, and confine ourselves to such things as instinct impels us to study.' The child, said Rousseau, should be given 'no verbal lessons; he should be taught by experience alone.'

The trouble with adults, Rousseau said, is that they are too eager to force their unnatural and arbitrary 'knowledge' into young minds. 'What is the use of inscribing on their brains a list of symbols which mean nothing to them?' he asked. Pupils might be able to repeat lists of facts, but they won't understand them; the facts sit in their memories, inert and useless, destroying their ability to think for themselves. Making children learn information alien to their personal experience represented an assault on their nature:

> *No, if nature has given the child this plasticity of brain which fits him to receive every kind of impression, it was not that you should imprint on it the names and dates of kings, the jargon of heraldry, the globe and geography, all those words without present meaning or future use for the child, which flood of words overwhelms his sad and barren childhood.*

Rousseau was an original thinker and a moving writer, and his argument that the natural curiosity of children is stifled by adult pedagogy became a multi-generational 'meme' – an idea that replicates itself. Throughout the next two centuries and into the current one, the story of Émile has been told and retold, in varying versions, using different language and with different reference points, but with the same underlying themes.

In the late nineteenth and twentieth centuries, a series of thinkers and educators founded 'progressive' schools, the core principle of which was that teachers must not get in the way of the child's innate love of discovery. Traditional academic subjects like history or languages or arithmetic were relegated in importance; after all, few children seem naturally interested in them. The emphasis was put on 'learning by doing' – hands-on experience, rather than verbal exchange. Instructional teaching was banned or limited, exercises in play and self-expression encouraged.

Maria Montessori's schools form the most celebrated example of the progressive philosophy in action; Larry Page and Sergey Brin, the founders of Google, both attended Montessori schools and credit the Montessori ethos as a contributor to their success. In the 1970s, Paulo Friere, an influential Brazilian education scholar, criticised teachers who 'filled' students with facts alien to their 'existential experience'. Rather than treating pupils like bank accounts in which we deposit information, he said, the job of education is to help children take responsibility for themselves.

The contemporary version of this progressive philosophy is associated with the phrase 'learning skills' (sometimes called 'higher order skills', 'thinking skills' or more recently, 'twenty-first century skills'). Montessori and her contemporaries believed passionately in education for its own sake. The proponents of 'learning skills' are more concerned with how schools prepare pupils for the world of work. They share the progressive belief that schools should spend less time on teaching specific knowledge of specific subjects. Instead, they argue, schools should focus on abstract skills like creativity, problem-solving, critical thought and curiosity. Such skills, it is said, will equip children for whatever the future throws at them.

It's a philosophy that has made its way deep into the educational mainstream. It can be found wherever you see an approving reference to pupils 'taking control of their own learning' or a teacher criticised for spending too much time on instruction instead of allowing children to express themselves. A report published on the website of a British teaching union states plainly, 'a 21st-century curriculum cannot have the transfer of knowledge at its core'.

In recent years, the learning skills cause has been joined by technological visionaries, hot with the entrepreneurial, do-it-yourself spirit of Silicon Valley. The age of Wikipedia and Google might have been conceived of by Rousseau in a dream. Any child with an iPad can explore the world's knowledge as she pleases, without the interference of teachers. The educational consultant Sir Ken Robinson says that children 'don't need to be helped to learn . . . They are born with a vast, voracious appetite for learning . . . it starts to dissipate when we start to educate them and force-feed them education.' Now that the web saves us from the task of memorising facts, schools can focus exclusively on developing their thinking skills.

The songs sound contemporary but the melodies would have been perfectly familiar to the first readers of *Émile*; industrialism is cast as the enemy (traditional schools are invariably described as 'factories'), and traditional categories of knowledge are regarded with suspicion. An emphasis on personal experience is accompanied by plangent paeans to the unhindered curiosity of children. The irony of 'twenty-first century skills' is that it represents an ideal of learning that first emerged when France had an emperor and America was a British colony.

Its proponents often fail to acknowledge their intellectual ancestry, which is odd but hardly unforgivable. What's less understandable is that their ideas have been proven false, repeatedly – shown to contradict everything modern science tells us about learning – yet are still discussed as if new, shiny and bursting with possibility. We now know that Rousseau was wrong. The curiosity of children does not work in anything like the way he believed, or his contemporary adherents propose. His ideas are seductive, but the reason they have to be constantly reinvented is that they do not work.

To understand why, let's start with three misapprehensions about learning common to supporters of 'curiosity-driven' education:

1. 'Children don't need teachers to instruct them.'

Those who think the natural curiosity of children is stifled by pedagogical instruction overlook something fundamental about human nature – as a species, we have always depended on the epistemic endowment of our elders and ancestors. Our generation didn't need to rediscover fire or how to build a skyscraper. Every scientist stands on the shoulders of giants, every artist works within or against a tradition. A baby learning language from the adults around her is the most recently formed link in what the educationalist Paul Harris terms an 'ancient tutorial system'.

The unusually long period for which children are dependent on adults is a clue that humans are designed to learn from others, rather than just through their own explorations. Though the extent and intensity of adult-child instruction varies, adults in every culture teach their offspring. Harris quotes a Kpelle father in Liberia: 'If I am cutting brush, I give him the machete for him to know how to cut brush. If work becomes hard, I'll show him how to make it easier.' The deliberate teaching of our young, rather than being a modern perversion of human nature, is part of our biological heritage. It was Rousseau, conceiving of Émile learning about the world in magnificent isolation, who denied human nature.

The weight of empirical evidence suggests that 'unguided learning' is something of an oxymoron. Richard Mayer, a cognitive scientist at the University of California, examined studies carried out from 1950 to the 1980s, comparing unguided learning with more traditional methods. In each case, children learned more and better under the old method of adult instruction than in the experimental classrooms. Mayer noted that the same ideas, under different names ('discovery learning', 'experiential learning', 'constructivism') recurred again and again over the decades, despite never having been shown to work.

Teachers aren't there just to provide direct instruction on what and how to learn, of course, but this is the core of what they should do. The researcher John Hattie synthesised over 800 meta-analyses (he ran a meta meta-analysis) of the success of different teaching approaches. The three most powerful teacher factors – those most likely to lead to student success – were feedback, quality of instruction and direct instruction. In other words, traditional teaching – the transmission of information from adults to children – is highly effective when skilfully executed. This ought to be obvious. But Hattie says that when he shows teacher trainees the results of his research they are stunned, because they have usually been told that direct instruction is a bad thing.

In the absence of knowledge imparted by adults, children's natural curiosity only takes them so far. Epistemic curiosity, as we learned at Babylab, is a state of being 'ready to learn'. Unless a child's readiness to learn is fed by knowledge, it can quickly fade. Students trying to learn science in the absence of direct instruction become discouraged and confused, or pick up misconceptions that harm their learning later. The internet doesn't solve this problem; it makes it worse. Imagine a group of children trying to learn about Darwinian evolution, for example, armed only with a broadband connection. How many would end up concluding that it is a Satanist plot? Some of them might learn some valuable information but only after wasting a lot of time struggling to distinguish spurious nonsense from informed discussion. Independent learning is a great goal. But if children are made to start there, most won't get much further.

Schools and teachers are also there to tell children *what* to learn – to direct them to stuff that they might find boring now but that we, as parents and as citizens, believe they ought to know. Childhood is a time when serendipity plays a large part in learning. Teachers can help children stumble across areas of knowledge that they didn't know they were interested in – unknown unknowns – and that they find dull or intimidating at first pass. How can you know you have a passion for the plays of Shakespeare if read the first pages of *Hamlet* and all you see is gibberish? A teacher who can decipher that gibberish, and persuade the child it is worth persisting with, can change someone's life. Children need to gain enough information to be conscious of their own information gaps, and sometimes that requires firm direction. Without it, we condemn them to be forever uninterested in their own ignorance.

Of course there are classrooms and schools in which the curiosity of children is suffocated by unimaginative teachers who make them learn facts without bothering to make those facts interesting. But to conclude from this that teacher instruction is, *in principle*, a bad thing, represents a wild leap in the wrong direction. If children are to become wise and skilful operators of the cultural survival vehicle into which they have been born, we need to help them locate the controls.

2. 'Facts kill creativity'

The TED conference makes all of its talks freely available online. It has hosted heads of state, rock stars, Nobel Prize-winning scientists and billionaires, but its most-viewed talk ever is by a genial middle-aged education consultant from Liverpool who was, until he spoke at TED, little known.

Sir Ken Robinson's 2008 talk on educational reform, entitled 'Do Schools Kill Creativity?' has now been viewed over four million times. In it, Robinson cites the fact that children's scores on standard tests of creativity decline as they grow older and advance through the education system. He concludes that children start out as curious, creative individuals but are made duller by factory-style schools which spend too much time teaching children academic facts, and not enough helping them express themselves. Sir Ken clearly cares greatly about the well-being of children, and he is a superb storyteller, but his arguments about creativity, though beguilingly made, are almost entirely baseless.

The Scottish Enlightenment philosopher David Hume pointed out that there is nothing particularly interesting about the idea of gold, or about the idea of a mountain. But a gold mountain? Now you have something. Creativity starts in combination. Progressive educationalists like Robinson frame existing knowledge as the enemy of new ideas. But at the most basic level, all of our new ideas are made up of old ones: to imagine a winged horse, you first need to be familiar with the ideas of horses and wings; to create a smartphone you need to know about computers and phones. The more existing ideas you have in your head, the more varied and richer will be your novel combinations of them, the greater your store of reference points and analogies. A fact is just a particular class of idea about the world, and it can be put to work in lots of different ways.

We romanticise the curiosity of children because we love

their innocence. But creativity doesn't happen in a void. Successful innovators and artists amass vast stores of knowledge, which they can then draw on unthinkingly. Having mastered the rules of their domain, they can concentrate on rewriting them. They mix and remix ideas and themes, making new analogies and spotting unusual patterns, until a creative breakthrough is achieved.

Researchers who study innovation have found that the average age at which scientists and inventors make breakthroughs has increased over time. As knowledge accumulates across generations, it takes longer to acquire it, and thus longer to be in a position to supersede or add to it.[*] Even geniuses have to accumulate knowledge of their field for years before they can produce masterpieces. Mozart, the archetypal child prodigy, was in the twelfth year of his career when he composed his first piece of enduring artistic value. As Steven Pinker puts it, 'geniuses are wonks'. Without knowledge, including factual knowledge, a child is like a sculptor with no clay to work with – she is creative, but only in theory.

Here are a few examples of people whose curiosity and creativity were fed by factual knowledge:

William Shakespeare went to the kind of school that would have horrified Sir Ken. Its pupils were made to learn, by way of repetition, over a hundred Latin figures of rhetoric. They were also expected to become familiar with texts

---

[*] See for example the paper 'Age and Great Invention', by Benjamin F. Jones.

that had little to do with their immediate experience, by ancient authors like Seneca and Cicero. We have no record of how much Shakespeare enjoyed school, but we have plenty of evidence that it didn't stifle his creativity. It's not just that he went on to produce the greatest body of creative work ever attributed to one person. It's that, as the Shakespeare scholar Rex Gibson put it, 'Everything Shakespeare learned in school he used in some way in his plays . . . his dramatic imagination was fuelled by what would now be seen as sterile exercises in memorisation and constant practice.'

A working-class boy who went to a demanding traditional school, **Paul McCartney** was a good student, excelling at English and Latin. By the time he joined The Beatles, he says, 'I had a love of literacy. With "Eleanor Rigby" I was trying to write like a good poet.'

In an 1844 letter to his friend J.D. Hooker, **Charles Darwin** makes it clear that his great insight emerged from the methodical accumulation of facts:

I was so struck with distribution of Galapagos organisms . . . that I determined to collect blindly every sort of fact which could bear in any way on what are species . . . I have never ceased collecting facts – At last gleams of light have come, and I am almost convinced (quite contrary to the opinion I started with) that species are not (it is almost like confessing a murder) immutable.

Jacob Rabinow, a prolific inventor with over 200 registered patents, was interviewed by the psychologist Mihaly Csikszentmihalyi about the requirements for creative thought. Rabinow thought the most important was 'a big database' of memorised knowledge: 'If you're a musician, you should know a lot about music . . . if you were born on a desert island and never heard music, you're not likely to be a Beethoven . . . You may imitate birds but you're not going to write the Fifth Symphony.' The earlier you start building your database, the better: 'So you're brought up in an atmosphere where you store a lot of information . . . The small differences at the beginning of life become enormous differences by the time you've done it for 40, 50, 80 years.'

Good teachers help to create this atmosphere. They actively direct the curiosity of children, helping them transform their diversive curiosity into epistemic curiosity, which in turn starts building the database that makes creativity possible.

3. 'Schools should teach thinking skills instead of knowledge'

In 1946 the Dutch psychologist and chess grandmaster Adriaan de Groot ran an experiment that changed the way scientists think about learning. He displayed a chess board to his subjects, with the pieces arranged as if a game was underway, for just a few seconds. He then asked them to reconstruct the position from memory. Grandmasters and masters were able to reproduce the positions with near-perfect accuracy. Good amateur players could only replace about half the pieces in the right positions, and novices managed only a third.

On the face of it, chess is a game of pure reasoning. But the core of chess ability is *knowledge*; chess masters have more positions stored in their memories and are thus able to instantly recognise more positions as they come up, which frees their conscious minds to focus on evaluating the next move (or the next several moves). William Chase and Herbert Simon replicated de Groot's experiment, adding a crucial twist. The players were shown not just real chess positions but random arrangements of pieces that would be impossible in an actual game of chess. The experts performed just as well as they had in de Groot's experiment with the real positions, but when it came to the scrambled positions, they performed no better than the amateurs.

Chess, rather than being about an abstract thinking skill, is highly knowledge-bound. Top players have tens of thousands of chess positions stored in their memory. Similar experiments have been repeated with experts from physics, algebra and medicine, always with the same results. When the task is changed to one that lies outside the expert's domain, they fail to transfer their skills to the new problem, because their skills are bound up with knowledge of that specific field.

Another way of putting this is that a mental skill is not the same as an algorithm – a process that can be applied to any problem, regardless of subject. 'Learning skills' grow organically out of specific knowledge of specific domains

— that is to say, facts (and I'm including here cultural knowledge, of the plot of *Hamlet*, for example). The wider your knowledge, the more widely your intelligence can range, and the more purchase it gets on new information. This is why the argument that schools ought to prioritise 'learning skills' over knowledge makes no sense; the very foundation for such skills is memorised knowledge.* The more we know, the better we are at thinking.

If the science of how the mind works has established one thing in the last fifty years, it is this — human memory isn't like computer memory, a place in which data can be stored and retrieved. It is central to the very act of thinking. *Long-term memory*, in particular, is the source of our intelligence, insight and creativity.

Our minds store information in one of two places: working memory (sometimes called short-term memory) and long-term memory. Working memory is what we can keep in our conscious minds at any one time. It is the brain's scratch-pad, the temporary mental space in which we perform acts of thinking, like arranging a sentence or doing a sum. It's rather cramped. We can only keep a few items in it simultaneously before one or more of them slip beyond recall; according to a landmark 1956 study by the cognitive psychologist George Miller, we can cope with about seven

---

* Of course, intelligence is much more than the memory of facts. But there is a fundamental symbiosis between the two. In the words of the writer Joshua Foer, intelligence and memory 'go hand in hand, like a muscular frame and an athletic disposition.'

numbers at once, and almost all information stored there is lost within thirty seconds if it is not rehearsed. When actually *processing* these elements rather than merely storing them – trying to do a sum with numbers, for example – most of us can only juggle two or three.

To boost our processing power we use something psychologists call 'chunking'. Given a sum – say 42 x 7 – we break the problem down into a few discrete chunks and manipulate them until we get to the answer. But it's hard because, first, you have to form one chunk (say, 40 x 7 = 280), and then you have to hold it in your working memory while you perform the next chunking operation (add 7 x 2 = 14), before finally adding the two together. Often, somewhere between those operations, one chunk drops out of our working memory and you have to start again. Or give up. If working memory was a piece of software we'd be tempted to take it back to the store and request an upgrade. Even when we use chunking, its limits make any act of multi-element thinking very difficult. Luckily, we have an extraordinary ability to cheat its constraints.

If working memory has the dimensions of a bedsit, long-term memory is the brain's giant underground warehouse. It's a space for everything we've picked up along the way: words, names, capital cities, card tricks, scientific ideas, Greek myths, the procedure for calculating the length of the hypotenuse or how to change a fuse. Some of these items take an effort to retrieve, but many can be summoned up effortlessly, instantly and intuitively. This facility greatly improves our ability to think. As an example of what I mean, give yourself five seconds to memorise the following string of 14 digits:

74830582894062

I'm guessing that you found this impossible; most people would, because you had to rely on your short-term memory. Now attempt the same with this string of 21 letters:

LUCY IN THE SKY WITH DIAMONDS

This time, you barely needed a second. The contrast is so striking that it seems like a completely different problem. But fundamentally it's the same. Both are strings of 'arbitrary symbols'; in one case numbers, in the other letters. The real difference is that one of them triggers a set of associations with knowledge stored in our long-term memory. We can chunk the letters into words we know, and we can chunk the words into a sentence we recognise as grammatical. We can chunk the whole phrase as the title of a song by The Beatles because of our background knowledge of popular culture. The knowledge we have stored deep in our database has made our thinking faster and easier.

Let's return to mental arithmetic. You can probably solve a problem like 22 x 11 with relative ease because you are able to use chunks of knowledge in your long-term memory; you know that 22 x 10 is 220 because you remember that anything multiplied by ten involves adding a zero to the end. So then all you need to do is add 22 to 220, and that's something your working memory can handle on its own. If you don't have such knowledge committed to long-term memory the whole process becomes much more arduous, even if you have learned the process of multiplication.

Long-term memory is the hidden power behind the throne of cognition. Without it, none of us would be able to cross a busy road, make an omelette or write an email. The more complex the mental operation, the bigger role it plays. When a tennis player selects a shot, an airplane pilot responds to turbulence, or a barrister constructs her argument, they are instinctually drawing on a storehouse of similar situations they have built up over years which enables them to instantly recognise the basic characteristics of the new situation and respond, without having to think it through from first principles.

Knowledge makes you smarter. People who know more about a subject have a kind of X-ray vision; they can zero in on a problem's underlying fundamentals, rather than using up their brain's processing power on getting to grips with the information in which the problem comes wrapped. In a classic experiment, Michelene Chi and her fellow researchers asked physics novices and experts to sort physics problems into categories. The novices sorted the problems according to their surface features – whether the problem featured a spring or an inclined plane. The experts classified the problems according to the physical law needed to solve it. Thinking skills like this can't be taught directly; they grow out of knowledge.

Critics of fact-based learning will sometimes ask, 'Why does it matter if a child knows the date of the Battle of Hastings?' It matters because facts stored in long-term memory are not islands unto themselves; they join up with other facts to form associative networks of understanding. Knowing the date of the Battle of Hastings enables you to place it, however roughly, in relation to, say, the date of the signing of the Magna Carta and the accession of Queen Elizabeth I to the throne. Once you have that kind of chronological scaffolding in place you can, as it were, forget it; it gets chunked into your long-term memory, freeing you to start grappling with deeper questions, like the evolution of English nationhood.*

---

* Joe Kirby, a London teacher and education blogger was shocked when he asked pupils about Second World War poetry, only to be asked: 'Sir, does that mean that there was a *first* world war?' Many of them had no idea who Churchill was, other than the nodding dog featured in an ad campaign for an insurance company. A colleague of Kirby's, teaching English in a disadvantaged school, found pupils were under the illusion that the English language was invented in the 1960s and that Shakespeare wrote the Bible. Lacking the building blocks of knowledge, these pupils will find it very hard to acquire thinking skills, or take a full part in the life of their society. Even relatively bright and well-motivated pupils are leaving school without knowing much about much. In 2009, a professor at one of Britain's top universities published the results of a survey of his first-year students, asking them basic questions about Britain's history. He was shocked by their ignorance. Eighty-nine per cent could not name a British prime minister from the nineteenth century. The participants in this survey were history undergraduates.

This is why curiosity, like other thinking skills, cannot be nurtured, or taught, in the abstract. Rather than being stifled by factual knowledge, it depends on it. Until a child has been taught the basic information she needs to start thinking more deeply about a particular subject, it's hard to develop her initial (diversive) curiosity into enduring (epistemic) curiosity; to get her to the stage where she is hungry for more knowledge about English history, and ready to ask her own, probing questions about it. Sir Ken Robinson has it precisely the wrong way around when he says that the natural appetite for learning begins to dissipate once children start to be educated. The curiosity of children dissipates when it *doesn't* get fed by knowledge, imparted by parents and teachers. Even when they find something interesting to begin with, children without adequate background knowledge of a subject will soon give up on learning about it, deciding that it's just 'not for me'. Knowledge gives curiosity staying power.*

Why doesn't the internet free us all from the onerous

---

* Once you grasp the role of background knowledge in thinking you can understand why school, for so many kids, is such a drag. Compared to educated adults, even bright children have a very small database of knowledge. So when they're asked to think about stuff at school, they're relying heavily on working memory without much support from long-term memory. As the psychologist and education expert Daniel Willingham says, thinking is 'slow, effortful and uncertain' when we don't know much. Teachers and schools often get the blame for the inevitable by-products of early learning: frustration and boredom.

responsibility of memorising the names of nineteenth-century prime ministers, or chemical elements, or the spelling of words? The question is based on the same fundamental misconception of how the brain works. When we search for information on the web we are deploying that blunt and limited instrument, working memory. The less we know in the first place, the more brain power we have to expend on processing, comprehending and remembering what we've just read, and the less we have left over to think and reflect on it. The emptier our long-term memories, the harder we find it to think. Anyone who stops learning facts for himself because he can Google them later is literally making himself stupid. Children who aren't encouraged by adults to commit information to their long-term memories are having their potential damaged and their desire to learn stymied. When we abandon them to the internet, we are leaving their epistemic curiosity to die.

The opposition that progressive thinkers make between knowledge and curiosity is not just false, it's harmful. It is most likely to hurt the children whom progressives often say they want to help most – those at the bottom of society.

The single most important contributor to future success, even for children aged six and younger, isn't a child's intelligence, but what she *knows*. A longitudinal study of 2,700 children funded by the US Department of Education followed the lives of its subjects for over a decade, from preschool or kindergarten onwards. The best predictor of academic achievement was general knowledge, such as vocabulary (the next best predictor was fine motor function; in third place came character traits like self-control and motivation).

It's nice to think that children will gain such knowledge by relying only on their innate desire to learn, but it's not true. Epistemic curiosity requires us to care about our own information gaps, and that means – as George Loewenstein realised – knowing something in the first place. The more knowledge children acquire early on, the better they are at learning, and the more they will *enjoy* learning. Just as start-ups need to borrow large amounts of capital to kick-start their growth, so children depend on knowledge transmitted by teachers to fuel their nascent intellectual curiosity.

Knowledge loves knowledge. As we've seen, new information that can't find any networks to affix itself slides out of the clutches of working memory within half a minute or so. If you are told for the first time that Thomas Jefferson died on 4 July, you're much more likely to remember that fact if you already know who Jefferson was, the role he played in America's birth, and the significance of that particular date. The more broad-ranging your general background knowledge, the stickier you are likely to find any new information. The wider your net, the more gets caught in it.

Start off with a small net, and you'll always be playing catch-up. Knowledge is subject to what sociologists call a 'Matthew Effect', named after a verse from the Gospel of Matthew: 'For whosoever hath, to him shall be given, and he shall have more abundance: but whosoever hath not, from him shall be taken away even that he hath.' In other words, the knowledge-rich tend to get richer while the knowledge-poor get poorer. A six-year-old student who knows a little less about how to read will find it harder to absorb knowledge from a book than her peers. When new information is introduced to the class, she will remember less of it than her classmates, *even if she's making the same effort* – because she has to devote more of her cognitive resources to dealing with the incoming information. Over time, as she falls behind in her class, she may get dispirited and stop trying.*

Minor differences soon become major ones. Daniel Willingham, a cognitive psychologist at the University of Virginia and an expert on learning, has performed a hypothetical calculation to demonstrate how the Matthew Effect works. Suppose Sara has ten thousand facts in her memory and Lucy has nine thousand, and they're both introduced to a new set of facts. Sara might remember ten per cent of the new facts, whereas Lucy remembers nine per cent. Now assume this is repeated nine times over the next nine months. By the end of it, the gap between Sara and Lucy will have widened from 1,000 facts to 1,043

---

* People making progressive-style arguments are fond of quoting W.B. Yeats: 'Education is not the filling of a pail, but the lighting of a fire.' Apart from being a good example of why the internet is an unreliable source of knowledge (Yeats never said or wrote any such thing) the metaphor actually reveals the blind spot of progressive thinkers. Fires need fuel to keep burning.

facts, and it will only keep widening unless Lucy makes an extra effort to catch up. But this is difficult, because Sara is pulling away from her at speed.

This is roughly the situation faced by kids who start school knowledge-poor, versus their knowledge-rich counterparts. The upside of the Matthew Effect is that it works both ways. If teachers and parents make an intensive effort to raise Lucy's knowledge levels, they can help her out of this vicious circle and into a virtuous one, in which the more she learns, the more she absorbs, and the more she *wants* to learn. Of course, if pupils attend a school in which teachers are discouraged from imparting knowledge directly, they won't get this help.

The evidence suggests that novices – students with comparatively low background knowledge – gain the most from adult instruction. A review of approximately seventy studies in the US found that highly skilled learners learn more with less guided instruction, whereas students who find learning difficult do significantly worse than they do under guided instruction.* When presented with an algebra problem, novices' only cognitive resource is working memory, because they're dealing with the various elements of the equation as if for the first time, so they need to lean on an external cognitive resource – a

---

* There is a significant additional finding. The less skilled learners who were allowed to study under the less guided approach tended to *like it* more, even though they learned less from it. Not having to learn stuff can make school more fun, but less valuable.

teacher – to work it through. Students who already have some knowledge of algebra can draw on an extra, internal resource – their long-term memory.[*]

Progressive education ideas are so called because they are anti-hierarchical – against the teacher as authority figure, or the concept of approved subjects – and a knowledge-rich education has somehow come to be seen as elitist. But progressive educational practices tend to entrench social hierarchies. They're better for more knowledgeable learners than less knowledgeable ones, and the more knowledgeable children are those, like Alexander Williams in Annette Lareau's study, who grew up in houses filled with books, with parents who enjoyed imparting knowledge to them – typically, middle-class kids. The problem is not that knowledge is elitist, but that the elites have a stranglehold on knowledge.

Antonio Gramsci, the Italian socialist and originator of the phrase 'speaking truth to power', was imprisoned for his opposition to Mussolini, and considered himself a staunch

---

* One rejoinder to criticisms of progressive methods is to note that Larry Page and Sergey Brin seem to be doing rather well for themselves these days. Of course it's true that there are highly successful adults who attended unconventional schools. But I suspect Page and Brin would have done well whatever school they went to. It's possible they may have thrived more at a Montessori school than they would have done at a traditional school (we'll never know) but even if so that actually points to a problem with progressive schools – they tend to be much better for the brightest kids from the most supportive families than they are for the less fortunate.

enemy of unearned privilege. When he saw progressive ideas about education taking hold in Italy, he wrote, 'The replacement of "mechanical" by "natural" methods has become unhealthily exaggerated . . . previously pupils at least acquired a certain baggage of concrete facts. Now there will no longer be any baggage to put in order . . . the most paradoxical aspect of it all is that this new type of school is advocated as being democratic, while in fact it is destined not merely to perpetuate social differences but crystallize them.'

In 1978 the education academic E.D. Hirsch was conducting research on reading comprehension at a community college in Richmond, Virginia, using the same assignments he had been using on his students at the University of Virginia. The community college students, most of them black, showed comparable levels of reading fluency and comprehension to the students at the university. But to Hirsch's surprise, they were utterly baffled by a passage about General Lee's surrender at Appomattox, one of the most famous events in American history. Hirsch had an epiphany; without access to a common stock of basic cultural facts and information, these students would always be at a disadvantage, no matter how smart or hard-working they were.

Hirsch made it his life's work to campaign for an education curriculum that puts the emphasis on the rigorous teaching of traditional subjects: literacy, maths, history, science, literature. This has led some to cast him as a conservative, and perhaps he is, but only in educational terms. As Hirsch says, there is 'an inverse relationship between educational progressivism and social progressivism'. Progressive education is a sure means of preserving society's status quo, whereas educational conservatism – teaching kids according to a common, knowledge-rich curriculum – provides 'the only means whereby children from disadvantaged homes can secure the knowledge and skills that will enable them to improve their condition.'*

Antonio Gramsci believed in speaking truth to power, but when it comes to education, the powerful already know the truth. Knowledge forms the bedrock of what the sociologist Pierre Bordieu termed 'cultural capital' – the shared reference points that smooth and deepen relationships between the powerful in any given society. That's why parents in the upper echelons of societies around the world send their children to expensive private schools specialising in knowledge-rich, teacher-led instruction in traditional subjects. Rather than ceding the field to those already in possession of cultural capital, surely our public education systems should be designed to spread it as widely as possible?

E.D. Hirsch likens background knowledge to oxygen – vital yet easily taken for granted. It is hard to realise just what a gift it is, and what a handicap it is not to have it. The flame of curiosity doesn't burn in a vacuum.

---

* After many years espousing an unfashionable cause, Hirsch is now winning the argument in America. His ideas underpin the Common Core curriculum, designed to equip all children with the basic knowledge they need to be well-rounded, successful individuals and good citizens. Over the last few years it has been adopted by almost every state.

To close this chapter I'll share a poignant example of how a knowledge-poor childhood can blight the life chances of the smartest and most curious of kids.

In his compelling book on education, *How Children Succeed*, Paul Tough combined first-hand reporting from American schools with evidence from academic research to argue that we have overestimated the extent to which successful learning depends on intelligence, and underestimated the importance of 'non-cognitive traits' – put simply, character. He focuses on the motivation to learn, in particular the trait of *persistence*. Tough cites the work of the psychologist Angela Duckworth, who has produced an impressive body of work to show how the achievement of children – and adults – is dependent on their levels of 'grit' – a combination of self-control, focus and ability to recover well from failure or disappointment. A test of a student's willingness to persist in a boring task is a much better predictor of achievement than a test of intelligence. The most successful students aren't necessarily the cleverest; they are the ones who don't give up.

Tough summarises his case like this: 'What matters most in a child's development . . . is not how much information we can stuff into her brain in the first few years. What matters instead is whether we are able to help her develop a very different set of qualities, a list that includes persistence, self-control, curiosity, conscientiousness, grit, and self-confidence.' Although coming from a very different intellectual background to progressive educators, Tough evokes their critique of knowledge-based teaching with that disparaging use of the verb 'to stuff'. But in his book, Tough tells a story which demonstrates the enduring importance of learning facts.

He reports on the inspiring success of the chess team at Intermediate School 318 in Brooklyn. The school serves a mainly poor African-American and Hispanic neighbourhood, and the great majority of its pupils are drawn from struggling, low-income families. You wouldn't expect its chess team to do well in national tournaments – indeed you might be surprised to learn that it has a chess team at all. But over the last ten years, teams from the school's fourth, fifth and sixth grades have been taking on and beating teams from the elite private schools who routinely dominate such competitions.

The person most responsible for the remarkable achievements of IS-318's chess team is a teacher called Elizabeth Spiegel. Spiegel spends hours with individual pupils going over games they have played, move by move, identifying where they went wrong or what they did right. She makes it clear that she expects great things from them, and they have risen to her challenge with exceptional efforts.

One of Spiegel's star players was James Black, an African-American boy from Brooklyn's impoverished Bedford-Stuyvesant neighbourhood. With Spiegel's help, James became a chess 'master' before the age of thirteen, one of only three African-Americans do so, and had won a national championship. Tough tells us about how Spiegel took on the challenge of preparing James for the entrance exam to Stuyvesant, New York's most selective state school. She was warned it was an impossible goal, not least by her vice-principal, who pointed out that it was unheard of for a pupil who had achieved consistently low scores on standardised statewide tests, as James had, to ace an exam for an elite school.

Spiegel elected to ignore such advice. She knew James was exceptionally intelligent and intellectually curious. She had seen how quickly he absorbed knowledge about the game of chess. With intensive tutoring, she believed James would make it. As she said to Tough, 'I figure with six months, if he's into it and will do the work, I can teach a smart kid anything, right?' Not just a smart kid, in fact, but a kid who had shown exceptional qualities of curiosity, application and persistence – of grit.

It's a story that demands a happy ending, a triumph over the odds. Apart from being emotionally satisfying, such an ending would support the argument of Tough's book – that the cultivation of character is the trump card in educational achievement. But Tough is an honest reporter, and, as he tells it, the story of Spiegel and James ends up suggesting something else; that while curiosity and grit are critical to educational achievement, they're worth little without knowledge.* As we've seen, chess at a high level

---

* I am indebted to E.D. Hirsch's review of Tough's book, in *Education Next*, for this point.

is an exercise in memory and pattern recognition. A chess master like James can see what is and isn't possible within a glance. But knowledge domains like literacy or geography are multi-faceted, nebulous and difficult to define, and they are dependent on each other – it's difficult to learn physics without maths, or history without language skills. It is nearly impossible to get good quickly at everything at once. As Tough himself remarks, doing well in an elite school exam 'requires the knowledge and skills that a student has accrued over the years, most of which is absorbed invisibly throughout childhood from one's family and culture.'

Although Spiegel spent hours outside of lesson time working with James on the test, and he applied himself with determination and diligence, he found it impossible to overcome his basic lack of knowledge. He couldn't locate Africa or Asia on a map or name a single European country, his vocabulary was narrow, his maths skills extremely limited. The fundamental holes in his early education meant he could hardly get started on more difficult questions.

James failed to gain entry to Stuyvesant, whose best chess players would have been no match for him, not because he lacked curiosity, or grit, or intelligence. He failed because, unlike middle-class kids, he hadn't been 'stuffed with information' from an early age.

The engine of his curiosity was running on empty.

As we've seen, childhood curiosity is a collaboration between child and adult. The surest way to kill it is to leave it alone.

Epistemic curiosity is not a 'natural' state of mind requiring only the removal of obstacles to flourish, but a joint project that needs to be worked at. Left to their own devices, including digital devices, children get misinformed, distracted and dispirited. This applies with particular force to the children that reformers like Sugata Mitra passionately want to help – the poor.

Mitra's work is fascinating and in many ways inspiring, but the conclusion he reaches is dangerously misguided. Knowing – in the sense of a richly populated long-term memory – is not obsolete; it's the source of our insight, creativity and curiosity. The fatal flaw in 'curiosity-driven' approaches to education is that knowledge drives curiosity as much as curiosity drives the acquisition of knowledge. We're not good at learning new information unless we're in a curiosity zone in the first place, and, especially at an early age, we rely on others to direct us there.

When it comes to education, curiosity is in the odd position of being undervalued and over-praised at the same time. On the one hand, school systems can over-emphasise exam performance and vocational preparation at the expense of instilling pleasure in learning. This is an important but much-acknowledged problem. A less obvious but just as insidious one stems from the assumption that a child's curiosity only needs to be unlocked for them to head off on amazing, enlightening intellectual journeys of discovery. It's nice to think so, but without schools to build their database of knowledge, many children can grow up fatally unaware

of what they don't yet know, uninterested in their own ignorance, and at a lifelong disadvantage to more knowledgeable
– and so more curious – peers. They will find themselves
on the wrong side of the curiosity divide – and when we let
that happen, we're allowing whole lives to shrink.

When the narrator of Saul Bellow's novel *The Dean's
December* overhears a dog barking into the night, he thinks
of it as a plea to expand his narrow canine understanding:
'For God's sake, open the universe a little more!' Knowledge, even shallow knowledge – knowing a little about a lot
– widens your cognitive bandwidth. It means you get *more*
out of a trip to the theatre or a museum, or from a novel, a
poem or a history book. It means you can glance at the first
few paragraphs of a story in the *The Economist*, grasp its
essentials, and discuss them later. It means you can engage
with the person next to you at lunch on a broader range
of topics, contribute meaningfully to more meetings, be
more sceptical of dubious claims, and ask better questions
of everyone you encounter. Whoever you are and whatever
start you get in life, *knowing stuff* makes the world more
abundant with possibility and gleams of light more likely
to illuminate the darkness. It opens the universe a little.

PART THREE
STAYING CURIOUS

CHAPTER 8

Seven Ways to Stay Curious

1. STAY FOOLISH

The two most influential creative businessmen of the last hundred years had a lot in common. Both were California-based pioneers who successfully imposed their own aesthetic tastes on the everyday lives of millions. Both used what the Harvard Business School professor Clayton Christensen terms 'disruptive technologies' to build enormous and enduring business empires. Both were driven and intense characters. Both exhibited a high 'need for cognition', and infused this characteristic into the culture of their companies – at least while they were alive.

Walt Disney, Chicago-born, moved to Kansas City as a young man and found a job with the Kansas City Ad Company, where he became interested in the new techniques of animation. After reading a book on the subject, Disney decided that 'cel' (celluloid) animation would soon supersede cut-out animation. Before long he had started his own business, making short cartoons called 'Laugh-O-Grams', which ran at local movie theatres. Soon, Hollywood beckoned. Together with his brother Roy, Walt moved there to set up the first Disney studio, in their Uncle Robert's garage.

In the 1920s, Disney's characters, including Oswald the Rabbit, became famous as movie-going took off around the States. *Steamboat Willie*, which introduced Mickey Mouse in 1928, was one of the first cartoons with synchronised sound. Disney won his first Oscar – for the Mickey Mouse series – in 1932. Towards the end of that decade he built a campus for the Disney studios at Burbank, where full-colour, feature-length spectaculars like *Snow White and the Seven Dwarves*, *Fantasia* and *Dumbo* were created.

The rise of television threatened to kill off the movie theatres and, with them, Disney's business. But Disney embraced this new and fast-spreading technology. He adapted established characters like Mickey, Donald Duck and Goofy to TV, and created new series from scratch, featuring non-animated characters like Davy Crockett. By the mid-1950s, Disney realised that it could take advantage of the trend towards destination tourism, and built his first theme park in Anaheim, California. His company led the way in new technologies like animatronics; visitors to the Illinois Pavilion at the New York World's Fair in 1964–1965 were greeted by a robot Abraham Lincoln, created by Disney engineers.

After Walt Disney died in 1966, the company foundered. It lost its knack for innovation, failing to create new properties to match the success of Mickey Mouse, or to take advantage of new technologies, like computer animation. Under new, aggressive management in the 1980s, it became financially successful again. But although it remained a massive, highly profitable company, and one of the world's most valuable brands, the Walt Disney corporation never quite recaptured the creative zest that made it a global colossus in the first place.

In 2006, Disney's board was joined by Steve Jobs of Apple, after Disney agreed to buy Pixar, the computer animation company of which Jobs was CEO and a major stockholder. In the fifteen years following the release of *Toy Story* in 1995, Pixar had become something like Disney was in the 1930s, combining creative and commercial dynamism. During that time, Disney had been distributing Pixar's films, while envious of its success and acclaim. Disney's chief executive Michael Eisner and Jobs were fiercely competitive with each other; it was only after Eisner left that Disney felt ready to accept that as it wasn't able to beat Pixar, it would have to buy it.

Jobs, like Walt Disney, started a business that would change the world from a Californian garage. In his case, it was his parents' garage; that was where he and the technical genius he had befriended, Steve Wozniak, hacked, fiddled and tweaked their way to a new kind of computer, one that was small enough, simple enough and handsome enough to sit in a person's home. By 1983, Apple was in the Fortune 500. After Jobs was ejected from the company he had built, in 1985, he became fascinated by the new digital animation techniques being pioneered at a small division of George Lucas's production company, Lucasfilm. Lucas agreed to sell that unit to him; it became Pixar. For years, Jobs wasn't sure what to do with Pixar. He just knew that he was curious about what it did.

Steve Jobs was a merely competent technician and, though highly intelligent, not a particularly original thinker. What made him exceptional were a ferocious will to succeed and a burning sense of epistemic curiosity. Jobs was interested in everything: the Bauhaus movement, the poetry of the beats, Eastern philosophy, the workings of business, the lyrics of Bob Dylan, the biology of the digestive system. A university tutor remembers his 'very enquiring mind . . . he refused to accept automatically received truths, and he wanted to examine everything himself.'* Jobs took a course in calligraphy while at university for no other reason than that it interested him.†

---

* Jeff Bezos, founder of Amazon, also has an exceptionally powerful sense of epistemic curiosity. When he was a child, his mother discovered him trying to take his crib apart with a screwdriver. As a teenager he started a summer camp for intellectually inquisitive children called 'the Dream Institute'. A *Washington Post* profile of Bezos describes its activities: 'The children read selections from books such as "Gulliver's Travels," "Dune" and "Watership Down." They studied black holes. They wrote simple programs on an Apple computer that made their names scroll down the screen.'

† It later prompted Jobs to pay close attention to the fonts used on the first Macs, which in turn ensured the presence of classical fonts on every home computer made since.

Jobs's curiosity was crucial to his ability to invent and reinvent himself and his businesses. He had significantly more epistemic breadth than most of his peers in the technology business, and when the internet started breaking down the divisions between industries, he was best placed to take advantage. At Apple, he brought together at least four disparate cultures in which he had become deeply immersed: 1960s counter-culture, the culture of American business entrepreneurs, the culture of design and the culture of computer geeks.* When the invention of MP3s made the spread of digital music inevitable, it was Jobs's personal interest in music that, as much as anything, enabled him to be the first to launch a successful MP3 player and the first legal music download service. It helped him not just to spot the opportunity, but talk to music business executives in terms they understood, and later to persuade rock stars like Bono to help him sell his products.

Jobs's intellectual fascination with the creative process made him take on Pixar and then stick with it even while it lost money. Throughout his life he retained the interest in novel ideas and techniques that the young Walt Disney showed at the Kansas City Ad Company. Disney's failure to replicate its early successes was partly due to its failure to

---

* A recurring pattern in the history of innovation is the combination of something with its inverse to form a single invention: the clawhammer joined nail removal with nail driving; the pencil was joined with the eraser. By combining the hitherto opposed roles of businessman and hippie, Jobs provided a walking example of the same pattern.

institutionalise the driving curiosity of its founder. Instead, it focused on making money from its existing assets. Jobs was unimpressed with Michael Eisner's failure, as he saw it, to investigate what was happening next door:

> *Pixar had successfully reinvented Disney's business, turning out great films one after the other while Disney turned out flop after flop. You would think the CEO of Disney would be curious about how Pixar was doing that. But during the twenty-year relationship, he visited Pixar for a total of about two and a half hours ... He was never curious. I was amazed. Curiosity is amazingly important.*

One of the most important and difficult questions for any organisation, especially those whose success depends on staying abreast of technological change, is how to inculcate a spirit of curiosity into its executives and employees – how to create and sustain communities of enquiring minds. There is no formula for creating a curious culture. But we can glean a few clues from the history of nation states.

Up until about 1700, China was, in the words of the historian Ian Morris, 'the richest, strongest, and most inventive place on earth'. Yet in the succeeding century the West raced ahead economically and intellectually, and continued to do so until the late twentieth century, while China languished. There is more than one reason that Europe, and then America, industrialised more quickly and successfully than China, as well as India and most other Asian countries; legal frameworks, education systems and natural resources all played their part. But one factor was that the West unlocked the power of human curiosity, while the East did not. The great Eastern empires suffered from what another historian, Toby Huff, calls a 'curiosity deficit'. The Chinese elites weren't interested in exploring the knowledge and technologies of the West because they were perfectly content as they were.

Although the seventeenth-century Catholic Church did its best to suppress Galileo's discoveries, it would be wrong to characterise it as intellectually incurious. Many men of the cloth were up to date with the latest thinking in the new sciences, and some were practitioners in their own right. After the publication of Galileo's *The Starry Messenger*, Cardinal Robert Bellarmine ordered the best mathematicians and astronomers at the Jesuit College to study it.

That it was Bellarmine who also presided over the Church's censure of Galileo in 1616 tells us something important. It wasn't that the Church was incurious about the true nature of the cosmos; it's that they believed such knowledge should remain the exclusive province of those who were able to handle it – that is, people like themselves. What made the authorities furious with Galileo wasn't just that he published *The Starry Messenger*, but that he published it in Italian, the language of the common man, rather than Latin, the language of elites.

In fact, it was Jesuits who took the Galilean telescope

to China and Thailand, and translated Galileo's work into Chinese. Matteo Ricci, a Jesuit who arrived in China in 1583, was a deeply learned man, and far from the stereotype of the arrogant Western missionary. He mastered written and spoken Chinese, and formed a close and enduring partnership with Xu Guangqi, a brilliant Chinese scholar who converted to Christianity. Together, the two men attempted to spark the interest of China's rulers and intellectuals in the astonishing new discoveries emerging from Europe. They made little headway.

Chinese scholars had been gazing at the heavens for hundreds of years, and are credited with the discovery of sunspots long before the Europeans. But their astronomical beliefs grew out of their spiritual and religious beliefs, rather than being founded on empirical observation. Ricci and Guangqi set about providing the tools needed to put Chinese astronomy on the same footing as European astronomy: trigonometric mathematics, planetary tables and the telescope.

They predicted eclipses with an accuracy that impressed the Chinese, and even staged competitions with Chinese astronomers to test the predictive power of their theories, which they would invariably win. Other missionaries showed the Chinese innovative military hardware. The reaction of the Chinese establishment to the news from Europe was, for the most part, a massive imperial shrug.

The Chinese authorities recognised that the Westerners had some impressive ideas and technology, but fundamentally, they weren't interested in it. China, under the Ming dynasty, was enjoying one of the most prosperous eras in its history. Its share of the world's economic activity far exceeded Europe's. Why should it care what the upstarts from Europe were doing when it had its own glorious traditions and a thriving economy?

'It is better to have no good astronomy than to have Westerners in China,' declared the great seventeenth-century Chinese scholar, Yang Guangxian. During previous periods of glory for Chinese civilisation, like the Han dynasty, he said, astronomers knew even less about the relationship between the sun and the moon than they do today. But still, 'the Han dynasty enjoyed dignity and prosperity that lasted for four hundred years.' Eventually, the Chinese told the Christians to go home, and to take their telescopes and cannons with them. China only fully accepted the premises of Western science in the twentieth century, and is only now making up the intellectual and economic ground it lost back then.

In his book *Why the West Rules – For Now*, Ian Morris argues that China's decline relative to the West has a lot to do with a simple geographical fact – the respective widths of the Atlantic and Pacific oceans. The Atlantic, 3,000 miles across, was 'a kind of Goldilocks Ocean' – it was just the right size. It was big enough that very different kinds of goods, springing from very different kinds of cultures, were produced around its shores, in Africa, Europe and the Americas, yet small enough that it could be traversed by Elizabethan galleons.

The Pacific, by contrast, was much too big to make trade possible or exploration feasible. The 8,000-mile gap between China and California was enough to prevent even the most intrepid Chinese from discovering and colonising the Americas before the Western Europeans. China was relatively safe from invaders and attackers, but it had fewer opportunities to explore the rest of the world and little incentive to do so.

Here was the root cause of China's curiosity deficit. In the seventeenth century, Europeans created a new market economy around the shores of the Atlantic, which focused Europe's greatest minds on understanding the movement of winds and tides, which led to the great unlocking of nature's secrets that came to be known as the scientific revolution. A broader intellectual and political revolution, now known as the Enlightenment, followed; it was Europeans, more familiar with other cultures, who were mostly likely to ask questions about what kind of society was a good society. Meanwhile, China looked inwards, to its ancient and unmatchably rich traditions, and was largely uninterested in the news brought to it by travelling Christians.

Success isn't good for curiosity. Like the Chinese in the seventeenth century, the managers of consistently profitable companies tend to look inwards, ceasing to be interested in ideas from beyond their own borders. The balance between *exploration* and *exploitation* becomes skewed too far towards the latter. Disney, despite its lack of world-beating new films, remained financially strong throughout its creatively fallow period. But its profit margin formed the equivalent of the Pacific Ocean; there was little incentive for it explore new ways of making or distributing Disney magic, when the current methods of exploiting it were generating so much cash.

Apple, during the long bull run of success it enjoyed after the return of Steve Jobs, maintained its pursuit of innovation partly because of the white-hot intensity of its chief executive's curiosity, and partly because its flirtations with demise over the previous decade meant it was not stupefied by overconfidence. Whether it can maintain its curiosity now that Jobs is gone and the company floats in a Pacific Ocean of cash is a question yet to be answered.

Another way of framing it is to ask how Apple, or any company, can remain aware of its own unknowns. The great physicist James Clerk Maxwell once remarked that 'thoroughly conscious ignorance is the prelude to every real advance in science.' Companies, and rulers, who learn to cultivate their 'conscious ignorance' – to be fascinated, even obsessed, by what they *don't* know – are the ones that are least likely to be caught unaware by change.

When he turned thirty, Steve Jobs was already musing about why it was that people his age and older began to develop rigid habits of thought: 'People get stuck in these patterns, like grooves in a record.' When Jobs was fifty, and had already come close to death from cancer, he told Stanford University's graduating students about Stewart Brand, a luminary of Californian counter-culture, and a technological visionary. Jobs finished his speech by repeating Brand's mantra: 'Stay Hungry, Stay Foolish.' 'I have always wished that for myself,' he said. He didn't leave instructions on how to instil the same attitude into a whole organisation.

2. BUILD THE DATABASE

My first real job after leaving university was at the London office of the advertising agency J. Walter Thompson. At that time, all new employees were handed two slim books, both authored by an agency alumnus, already long dead. His name was James Webb Young. The first book was called *How to Become an Advertising Man.** Although we sniggered at the dated style ('Salesmanship is the art of influencing any kind of human behaviour by putting the proposition in terms appealing to the other fellow') we all read it from cover to cover. Its advice was shrewd, cogently expressed and still pertinent.

Young worked on Madison Avenue just prior to its *Mad Men* heyday. He was of an older generation to Don Draper, having already attained a reputation as a master of persuasion by the time America entered the Second World War. When the American government approached him to ask if he would design a propaganda programme with the aim of depressing German morale, Young drafted a memo that

---

* On each of our copies the last word was crossed out with a marker pen and replaced by a scrawled 'person'.

displayed a characteristic blend of chutzpah, hard logic and no-nonsense practicality. He defined the challenge as if it were an exercise in soap powder marketing; the government needs 'an idea . . . that will bring us the most profit from the market in which we are to sell it — that is, the one that will secure the greatest lowering of morale in the shortest time, and meet with the least resistance . . . from prospective customers. In my opinion this idea is now The Inevitability of Defeat.'

The second book we were handed was called *A Technique for Producing Ideas*. Written in 1960, when Young was in semi-retirement, the book was intended for advertising people, but its lessons are widely applicable. In its modest way, it negates the need for any other books about the process of creative thinking. It is very short — pamphlet-sized — and immensely practical. There are no reflections on the ineffable mysteries of creative genius, no jargon and few digressions. It gives pride of place to curiosity.

Young's technique consists of five steps. The first is to 'Gather raw material'. By this Young meant knowledge about the product and its consumers. You might *think* there is nothing new to say about your product or the people who buy it, he says, but persist: look harder, and you will *see*. Young quotes Guy de Maupassant, who was told by an older writer to: 'Go out into the streets of Paris and pick out a cab driver. He will look to you very much like every other cab driver. But study him until you can describe him so that he is seen in your description to be an individual, different from every other cab driver in the world.' This was gathering of knowledge specific to the product and its consumers. Of equal importance to this, says Young, is 'the continual process of gathering of general materials':

> *Every really good creative person in advertising whom I have ever known has always had two noticeable characteristics. First, there was no subject under the sun in which he could not easily get interested — from, say, Egyptian burial customs to modern art. Every facet of life had fascination for him. Second, he was an extensive browser in all sorts of fields of information . . . In advertising, an idea results from a new combination of specific knowledge about products and people with general knowledge about life and events.*

Young's formulation is simple but powerful. Any task or project that requires creative thought will be better addressed by someone who has deep knowledge of the task at hand, and general background knowledge of the culture in which it and its users (or readers, or viewers) live. A mind well-stocked with these two types of knowledge is much more likely to be a fertile source of the serendipitous collisions that lead to brilliant ideas. Leo Burnett, founder of the global ad agency network that still bears his name, and a near-contemporary of Young's, said, 'Curiosity about life in all its aspects, I think, is still the secret of great creative people.'

Great ideas don't just spring from the moment of the

mental effort involved in trying to come up with one. Their roots extend back months, years, decades into their author's life; they are products of long-formed habits of mind as much as they are of flashes of brilliance. As Young puts it, 'To some minds each fact is a separate bit of knowledge. To others it is a link in a chain of knowledge.' It's clear that he intuitively understood the principle we examined earlier – that new knowledge is assimilated better, and has more creative possibility, the bigger the store of existing knowledge it is joining. Knowledge loves knowledge.

Highly curious people, who have carefully cultivated their long-term memories, live in a kind of augmented reality; everything they see is overlaid with additional layers of meaning and possibility, unavailable to ordinary observers. The fashion designer Paul Smith says that 'I've got eyes that see. A lot of people have eyes that look but don't see. I'll see something light next to something dark, or something smooth next to something rough, or Harris tweed next to silk, and that means something to me. I can look at architecture and the proportions of doors and windows and see pockets and the openings of a jacket. Or I listen to music that is very calm but has a very bright bit and that can be a navy blue suit with a flowery shirt to me.'

The rest of Young's steps depend and elaborate on his first. The second step is 'the working over'. This involves taking the facts you have gathered and looking at them again from different angles, bringing them into unusual combinations with other facts, constantly seeking interesting new relationships, new syntheses. This won't necessarily yield any good ideas; in fact Young predicts that you will hit a wall of hopelessness, when nothing fits, no insights present themselves, and everything you've learned is in a meaningless jumble in your mind. Your arrival at this hopeless point, says Young, is actually good news; it means this stage is over and the next one can begin.

This one involves, reassuringly, 'absolutely no effort of a direct nature'. It is the stage at which the unconscious is allowed to go to work, assisted only by the stimulation of something completely irrelevant to the task at hand. Young reminds the reader that Sherlock Holmes often drags Watson off to a concert in the middle of case, overruling the objections of his literal-minded partner, knowing that, having done the hard work of thinking, insight is now more likely to be discovered while the conscious mind is occupied by something else entirely.

The fourth and most magical stage takes place in the mind's subterranean chambers. After the concert, advises Young, retire to bed, and 'turn the problem over to your unconscious mind and let it work while you sleep.' Now that the conscious mind has prepared the ground, insight will take you unawares: 'While shaving, or bathing, or most often when you are half awake in the morning.' In the fifth and final stage, the idea is prodded, tested, tweaked and massaged into reality.

*

We all know about 'eureka moments', when ideas seem to drop unbidden into their creator's head. In fact, as Young knew, there is little accidental about such insights. They arise from the *gathering* and the *working-over* — the slow, deliberate, patient accumulation of knowledge.

As a young man, the great French mathematician Henri Poincaré worked as an engineer, and was sometimes asked to investigate mining disasters. He had been struggling with a problem in pure mathematics when he was summoned to the site of a mine to perform an inspection. He later recalled that the excursion allowed him to forget the problem altogether for the first time in several months. His unconscious, however, was just getting to work:

> *Having reached Coutances, we entered an omnibus to go some place or other. At the moment I put my foot on the step the idea came to me, without anything in my former thoughts seeming to have paved the way for it, that the transformations I had used to define the Fuchsian functions were identical with those of non-Euclidean geometry. I did not verify the idea; I should not have had time, as, upon taking my seat in the omnibus, I went on with a conversation already commenced, but I felt a perfect certainty. On my return to Caen, for conscience's sake, I verified the result at my leisure.*

Poincaré reflected that what had seemed, at the time, to be a fruitless accumulation of mathematical ideas was, in fact, essential preparation for his epiphany. In his unconscious, the ideas had become 'mobilized atoms' which collided into each other, arranging and rearranging themselves into ever more complex combinations until finally the 'most beautiful' of them made it into consciousness, just as he was boarding a bus.

In recent years, scientists have been examining the neural mechanics of the semi-conscious or unconscious creativity that artists and inventors from Kafka to Edison have relied on for inspiration. They have found that REM (rapid eye movement) sleep, when our dreams are most vivid, does indeed boost our creativity. The reason seems to be that this is when the brain feels most free to make connections between different associative networks of knowledge.

This is something else that Rousseau and his followers got wrong. When we learn facts, they don't just sit in our unconscious, inert and isolated, useless until recalled. They make themselves available for all sorts of tasks the conscious mind would never think of using them for. Sleep seems to work on our long-term memories like alcohol at a party. As the conscious mind releases its grip on thinking, the facts stored in our memory feel more free to talk to each other – to strike up relationships with bits of knowledge from outside their neighbourhood. When, during the day, the mind's resources are mobilised in the service of a particular problem, it's this after-hours mingling that often summons the final breakthrough.

Human memory is inefficient and unreliable in comparison to machine memory, but it's this very unpredictability that's the source of our creativity. It makes connections we'd never consciously think of making, smashing together atoms that our conscious minds keep separate. Digital databases cannot yet replicate the kind of serendipity that enables the unconscious human mind to make novel patterns and see powerful new analogies, of the kind that lead to our most creative breakthroughs. The more we outsource our memories to Google, the less we are nourishing the wonderfully accidental creativity of our unconscious.

Although creative people often find insight in dreams, it's a mistake to think that dreaming is necessarily a creative act in itself. The education writer and teacher Daisy Christodoulou cites the example of a school in which pupils were asked to 'think like designers' and encouraged to daydream. As she points out, there's a big difference between an expert's daydream and a novice's daydream. Expert designers have a huge store of background knowledge and learned processes, which feed into their dreams.

In the concluding section of his book, James Webb Young returns to where he started – the importance of lifelong curiosity. 'There is one [step] on which I would place greater emphasis – the store of general materials in the idea-producer's reservoir . . . the principle of constantly expanding your experience, both personally and vicariously, does matter tremendously in any idea-producing job.' Building the database is the surest route to producing ideas that will some day become part of someone else's database.

3. FORAGE LIKE A FOXHOG

If you have a knowledge-based career, you need a learning strategy. Is it best to be a specialist or a generalist – to know a lot about a little or a little about a lot?

The story of the last century has been one of increasing rewards to specialists. It's not enough for an historian to be expert on the civil war; she must be an expert on civil war marching songs. Today, Don Draper couldn't just introduce himself to clients as an ad man, but as a specialist in social media or branded content. Silicon Valley firms aren't just competing to hire the most brilliant software engineers but the ones most expert in coding for iOS or Android apps.

But the digital revolution – or rather the series of revolutions wrought by digital, wired technologies – has created a counter-trend. Paola Antonelli is senior curator in the department of architecture and design at the Museum of Modern Art in New York. Curators, she told me, come in two types: conservers and hunter-gatherers. She plants herself firmly in the latter category.* Antonelli is a self-proclaimed generalist, interested in gathering and synthesising different materials from disparate fields, from design and architecture to science, technology and philosophy. She describes herself

* Antonelli told me that she borrowed the distinction from one of her predecessors at MoMA, Emilio Abasz.

as 'a curious octopus. I am always reaching out and taking in things from everywhere.'

Antonelli told me that designers increasingly find themselves working in groups, and have to quickly adapt to other forms of knowledge. There are few design specialisms left, she says – some book designers design only books, but they are exceptions to the rule. Today's designers might find themselves working with engineers, marketers and accountants. 'For instance,' says Antonelli, 'if you are a branding designer and you are hired by a Texan oil company to create their corporate identity, you'll need to put a team together that includes an expert on oil production – and you'll need to be curious about the process of getting oil out of the ground. Unless you do that, you probably won't come up with the right answer.'

The spread of digital technologies into more and more areas of our lives is blurring the boundaries between domains: 'Increasingly, designers are having to think in terms not just of material objects but experiences and interactions,' says Antonelli. Designers now have to be more versatile than ever, and that means being curious about the knowledge of other people. If you want to succeed in today's music industry, you need to understand social networks; if you want to make a name for yourself in linguistics, you need to get to grips with data analytics.

Even sport, often thought of as purely physical domain, is increasingly knowledge-rich, and requires multi-disciplinary competence. For instance, to be a successful football manager

today, you need to have accumulated a deep knowledge of
tactical formations and some knowledge of statistical techniques, psychology – even economics. It used to be thought
that the only real requirement for a manager was to have been
a successful player. But increasingly the coaches of Europe's
biggest clubs are men whose playing careers were truncated
through injury, or simply because they weren't good enough.
When the Real Madrid and Chelsea manager José Mourhino,
himself an example of this trend, was asked why this was, he
replied: 'More time to study'.*

We know that new ideas often come from the cross-fertil-
isation of different fields, occurring in the mind of a widely
knowledgeable person. Francis Crick, discoverer of DNA,
trained as a physicist and later claimed that it was this back-

---

* Sir Alex Ferguson, probably the greatest manager British football has ever
known, also started young (he became manager of St Mirren aged thirty-
two). A former shipbuilder who never went to university, Ferguson has an
exceptionally hungry mind. In the course of his managerial career he became an expert in wine, horse-racing, the life of Abraham Lincoln and the
American Civil War. He is a film enthusiast and a voracious reader, who
has completed all five volumes of Robert Caro's monumental biography of
Lyndon Johnson. To put it mildly, this breadth of interest is not the norm
in football circles. While Ferguson is rightly lauded for his will to win and
motivational ability, his epistemic curiosity surely contributed to his success.
During his decades at the top, the game changed radically, but Ferguson
always adapted. When innovations like statistical analysis were introduced to
football, many managers of his generation ignored them, preferring to stick
to what they knew. Presumably Ferguson treated them as something else to
learn about.

ground that gave him the confidence to solve a problem biologists regarded as fundamentally insoluble. Picasso combined African sculpture with Western painting to create a new kind of art.

In the marketplace for talent, the people most in demand will always be those who offer an expertise few others possess. But having a breadth of knowledge is increasingly valuable too. These two trends exist in tension with each other. So should you focus on learning more about your own niche, or on widening your knowledge base?

This question recalls the story of the hedgehog and the fox. It's been told in many forms through the ages but the essence of it is always the same. The fox evades his attackers in a variety of inventive but exhausting ways, while the hedgehog adopts one tried and trusted strategy – hunkering down and letting its spikes do the work. In the words of Greek poet Archilochus: 'The fox knows many things, but the hedgehog knows one big thing.'

The philosopher Isaiah Berlin proposed that all thinkers could be divided into one category or another. There are thinkers who look at the world through the lens of one particular idea, and those who revel in a variety of perspectives. Plato was a hedgehog, Montaigne a fox. Tolstoy thought he was a hedgehog, but couldn't help writing like a fox. You can apply this distinction to people in politics or business. Ronald Reagan was a hedgehog, Bill Clinton a fox. Steve Wozniak was a hedgehog, Steve Jobs a fox, which may explain why they worked so well together.

The thinkers best positioned to thrive today and in the future will be a hybrid of these two animals. In a high-information, highly competitive world, it's crucial to know one or two big things and to know them in more depth and detail than most of your contemporaries. But to really ignite that knowledge, you need the ability to think about it from a variety of eclectic perspectives and to be able to collaborate fruitfully with people who have different specialisms.

For example, Charles Darwin knew as much about the life cycle of earthworms and the beaks of finches than anyone alive. But it was his reading of the economist Thomas Malthus that enabled him to rise above other naturalists and construct an overarching theory of life. If Darwin had read widely but hadn't built deep expertise in biology he would never have arrived at his big idea (and even if he had, he wouldn't have persuaded anyone of it). If he hadn't been such a voracious consumer of knowledge from other fields, he might not have come upon the insight that enabled him to see the underlying logic of evolution. Darwin was the archetype of a species he wouldn't have recognised – the foxhog.

Charlie Munger, Warren Buffett's business partner and vice-chairman of their legendary investment company Berkshire Hathaway, is one of the most successful investors of all time. He knows as much about picking stocks as anyone in the world and has an unbeatable depth of experience in buying and selling them. But that doesn't explain his pre-eminence – there are others, albeit not many, with similar expertise. What has elevated Munger above his peers is that he hunts for knowledge like a foxhog. He is constantly reading beyond his own field, in an effort to frame and reframe the information he receives. Munger is a passionate believer in the importance of working with what he calls 'multiple models'. When Munger looks at a business, he does so through lenses from maths, economics, engineering, psychology and other disciplines. Using multiple models is crucial, says Munger, because they give you different answers to everyone else, even when you are all looking at the same data. They turn facts into stories and information into insight. Breadth is as important as depth: 'Before you're going to be a great stock picker,' says Munger, 'you need some general education'.

The foxhog possesses what IBM calls 'T-shaped' knowledge. The most valuable 21st-century workers combine deep skills in a specialty (the vertical axis of the T), with a broad understanding of other disciplines (the horizontal axis). The former allows them to execute projects that require particular expertise; the latter enables them to see contextual linkages to other disciplines. Having a core competency differentiates the foxhog in the marketplace – it gives her a USP within her organisation and beyond it – while the top line of the T enables her to constructively link up with colleagues from different fields, and to adapt to different challenges throughout her career.

For a contemporary example of a successful foxhog, look no further than Nate Silver, the statistician and writer. Silver first gained recognition for developing a system for forecasting the performance of major league baseball players. But his interests always ranged far beyond sport, and when the 2008 presidential election came into view he started a blog on it, called 538.com (five hundred and thirty-eight being the number of votes in the US electoral college). At 538 he applied his statistical know-how to the business of analysing and predicting results in the party primaries and, later, the general election, with impressive accuracy. After being hired by the *New York Times* he did the same thing in 2012, and famously bested more traditional pundits by calling the final results with near-perfect precision. In 2013 he was poached by the ESPN network, where he applies statistical techniques to a variety of fields from sports to politics to the movies.

There may be more sophisticated statisticians than Silver in the world. But what makes him stand out is his ability to combine his statistical expertise with interest in and knowledge of different fields. That means he can offer a distinctive and often more valuable kind of analysis to those already available. Silver told the *Harvard Business Review* that he's an advocate for the kind of education that produces foxhogs: 'The thing that's toughest to teach is the intuition for what are big questions to ask. That intellectual curiosity . . . if you're going to have an education, then have it be a pretty diverse education so you're flexing lots of different muscles . . . You can learn the technical skills later on, and you'll be more motivated to learn more of the technical skills when you have some problem you're trying to solve or some financial incentive to do so. So not specializing too early is important.'

Western policy-makers, spooked by the success of Asian education systems in producing scientists and engineers, and worried about their economic competitiveness, have been insisting that our schools and universities focus on producing hedgehogs – specialists who can slot neatly into the job market when they graduate. But this is to see only one half of the equation. Educators in the most advanced Asian economies know that the kind of broad, cross-disciplinary education in which the best Western universities have traditionally excelled will be as valuable in the twenty-first century as it was in the twentieth. Here is Professor Tan Chorh Chuan, president of the National University of Singapore:

One thing I've been increasingly convinced about is the importance of intellectual breadth. There are two reasons why. First, many of the problems we face in our work and lives are complex. They cut across different disciplines and domains of knowledge. If you don't have a broad intellectual base, you will not be able to see the potential cross-disciplinary implications. Second, where we expected to do three or four jobs in a lifetime, the average graduate today might do 10 or 12. These jobs can cross many different sectors so you must have the intellectual base from which you can retool yourself more easily to do different types of work.

Discussions of the hedgehog and the fox often come down to whether it's better to be one or the other. But in a world that rewards expertise and also the groundbreaking insights that come from the clash of domains, we need to be both. We need to be foxhogs.

4. ASK THE BIG WHY

On 26 March 2007 two men sat down side by side and read out prepared statements as millions of people around the world watched on TV. Ian Paisley, Northern Ireland's hard-line and outspoken Protestant leader, and Gerry Adams, a Catholic, reputed to be the former commander of the Irish Republican Army, were sworn enemies. Each embodied the most uncompromising element of two sides that had been locked into a conflict stretching back decades, claiming thousands of lives, and ripping apart countless families. Yet here they were, almost unbelievably, not only sharing a table, but pledging mutual cooperation.

Somewhere in the room, out of range of the cameras, was a man who can claim to be one of a handful of those most responsible for bringing this ancient and once thought intractable dispute to an end. Jonathan Powell was Tony Blair's chief of staff throughout Blair's time as prime minister, and the UK government's principal negotiator in

Northern Ireland. In his book about the peace process, *Great Hatred, Little Room*, he recounts a seemingly endless series of meetings with the key players over a period of ten years, some of them taking place in great rooms of state in London or Ireland, others, more clandestine and more dangerous, in suburban houses, or churches deep in the heart of fiercely Republican communities – not the kind of places to be seen carrying a briefcase with the royal crest on it.

Powell is tall and thin and retains boyishly curly hair in his middle age. He is likeable – his eyes crinkle when he smiles – but brisk, talking and thinking at a disconcertingly fast pace. He is also direct; despite being a diplomat by trade (and author of an admiring book on Machiavelli) he comes across as someone who is far more likely to offend you than lie to you. This is probably a useful quality in his current job, because to succeed in it, he needs to be trusted by people who trust nobody.

Powell heads an NGO whose purpose is to mediate between governments and terrorist organisations. For reasons of politics and security, politicians and diplomats are usually unwilling to meet terrorists but usually realise that they need to communicate with them if they are find a permanent end to a long-running conflict. Powell offers governments a secret channel to these underground organisations, shuttling back and forth between the two sides until they are prepared to meet directly.

When I spoke to him he told me he was currently involved

in eight different conflicts around the world.[*] He had just returned from a holiday in Cornwall with his family, which he'd been forced to interrupt to fly to South America.[†] Powell couldn't tell me about the details of his work. But he was happy to discuss what I wanted to talk to him about – the role of curiosity in negotiation.

In their book *Negotiation Genius*, the Harvard Business School professors Deepak Malhotra and Max H. Bazerman tell the story of an American businessman they call 'Chris', whose firm was negotiating with a European company to purchase an ingredient for a new healthcare product. The two firms had agreed a price but become deadlocked over the question of exclusivity; the Europeans would not accept the Americans' demand that the ingredient not be sold to any of their competitors. The American negotiators offered more money, but their counterparts would not budge. As a last resort, the Americans called Chris and asked him to fly over to Europe and join the meeting. Malhotra and Bazerman describe what happened next:

---

[*] Powell's work means spending a lot of time with people who specialise in killing civilians. 'It must be quite . . . edgy?' I suggested. 'It can be very dangerous, yes,' he said.

[†] It may not have been coincidence that, shortly after our conversation took place, news emerged that the FARC terrorist organisation and the Colombian government launched their first direct peace talks in a decade.

When Chris arrived and took a seat at the bargaining table, the argument over exclusivity continued. After listening briefly to the two sides, he interjected one simple word that changed the outcome of the negotiation . . . The word was 'why'.

Chris simply asked the supplier why he would not provide exclusivity to a major corporation that was offering to buy as much of the ingredient as he could produce. The supplier's answer was unexpected: exclusivity would require him to violate an agreement with his cousin, who currently purchased 250 pounds of the ingredient each year to make a locally sold product. With this information in hand, Chris proposed a solution that helped the two firms quickly wrap up an agreement: the supplier would provide exclusivity with the exception of a few hundred pounds annually for the supplier's cousin.

Chris's colleagues hadn't asked the question, probably because they assumed that they already knew the answer; they hadn't thought hard enough about the possibility of unknown unknowns. As the negotiation expert Diane Levin has pointed out in a commentary on this story, they may have also been inhibited by social pressures. Asking penetrating questions can be construed as bad manners. It can make us feel exposed to accusations of stupidity. But according to texts on negotiation, asking 'why' is crucial to the unravelling of knotty conflicts. Richard Shell, author of *Bargaining for Advantage*, lauds the 'relentless curiosity' of experienced negotiators. In a classic work, *The Making of a Mediator*, Bernard Mayer and Alison Taylor recommend 'a commitment to curiosity and exploration'.

When it comes to negotiation (and mediation), Jonathan Powell isn't a fan of curiosity for its own sake: he cautions against the asking of endless, purposeless questions. But he points out that if each party accepts the other's negotiating position on its own terms, then the most likely result is deadlock. The key, he told me, is to ask what lies beneath the demand. 'The fundamental question,' Powell told me, 'isn't "what", it's "w*hy*".'

If the parties negotiate on their pre-agreed positions, the negotiation becomes a trade-off in which one side loses while another one gains. 'But,' Powell said, 'if you ask what people's underlying interests are – what do they *need* – then you're more likely to get to find an imaginative solution.' That means asking probing, penetrating questions which force the other party off their prepared script, and encourage them to open up about the pressures on them from their own side. It also means listening intently to their answers.

It sounds simple. But over and again, Powell said, negotiators make the same mistake. 'What always amazes me is that people go into these meetings without really attempting to understand the mindset of the people they're negotiating with. Good negotiators are intelligent listeners – they don't just hear out the other side and then present their positions. They listen carefully and try to understand where the other guys are coming from.'

The attitude Powell describes here has been termed, in

the context of doctor-patient relationships, 'empathic curiosity'. Dr Jodi Halpern, a bioethicist at the University of California, was once a practicing psychiatrist*. She noticed the way that patients seemed to respond better to doctors who seemed genuinely interested in them, rather than doctors who – following professional convention – remained emotionally detached in an attempt to be objective. She also noticed that even doctors who expressed genuine *sympathy* for their patients sometimes had trouble understanding or responding to their real needs. In 2001 she wrote an influential book arguing that empathy is more important than sympathy, because empathy involves making an effort to be *consciously curious* about the patient's perspective. 'Most people have the human capacity for empathic curiosity, for genuine interest in and emotional responsiveness to another person's perspective, but they can turn it on and off,' said Halpern. Doctors too often turn it off.

So, according to Powell, do negotiators. Decision-makers in business or government tend to assume that the goal of a negotiation is a result in which everyone's costs and benefits become roughly equal. But long-running disputes are often rooted in an underlying moral and emotional conflict that isn't susceptible to material negotiations. Only by applying 'conscious curiosity' can a negotiator or mediator identify

---

* Halpern uses the term *emphatic curiosity* in reference to clinical practice. In this book I use it in a broader sense, as interest in the thoughts and feelings of others, though obviously the two uses are congruent.

the contours of these deeper motivations, and thus search for ways to address them.

From 2004 to 2008, the social psychologist Jeremy Ginges and the anthropologist Scott Atran surveyed nearly 4,000 Palestinians and Israelis across the political and social spectrum, including refugees, Hamas supporters and Israeli settlers on the West Bank. They asked the participants to react to a series of hypothetical but realistic peace deals. Almost everyone on both sides rejected the deals outright. Asked to explain why, they would say that the values involved were sacred to them. Many Israeli settlers said that they would never consider trading any land on the West Bank, which they considered to have been granted by God. Palestinians considered the right of return to be sacred rather than something that might be traded for a concession from the other side.

The psychologist Philip Tetlock has called this effect 'the taboo trade-off'. When parties in a negotiation are asked to trade something they consider sacred for something secular or material, they become angry, inflexible, and deaf to dry cost-benefit reasoning. Indeed, material offers can backfire. Contrary to classical economic theory, financial incentives can make people even less likely to make concessions, compared to when an offer includes no such money.

When Atran and Ginges added monetary incentives to their hypothetical deals – for instance, an offer of $10 billion a year to the Palestinians – the respondents being offered the incentive reacted with even greater outrage than before. The researchers also spoke to leaders on both sides of the dispute, and found that financial proposals elicited a similar response even from these experienced negotiators: 'No, we do not sell ourselves for any amount,' a Hamas leader angrily told the researchers after they suggested adding in American aid to the deal.

Atran and Ginges found that the only proposals appearing to break the deadlock were symbolic ones, which carried a great emotional freight. Palestinian hard-liners were more willing to consider recognising the right of Israel to exist if the Israelis offered an official apology for the displacement of Palestinians in the 1948 war. Israeli respondents were prepared to consider borders very close to those that existed before the 1967 war if Palestinian groups explicitly recognised Israel's right to exist.

Western mediators, operating on the rational actor principle, find such attitudes hard to come to terms with. Politicians sometimes talk about taking a 'businesslike' approach to such disputes, or argue that peace will inevitably follow progress on material issues, like jobs or access to the electricity supply. Making progress on such issues can certainly help, but it can also throw into even sharper relief conflicts of values – values rooted in fierce, heartfelt beliefs about identity and moral purpose. If answers are to be found, they lie buried deep in the 'why' of the dispute rather than the 'what'. Only negotiators curious enough about the other side's fundamental beliefs and feelings will discover them.

In Northern Ireland, said Powell, 'we spent a long time

knocking our heads against the issue of decommissioning
[the disarming of the IRA]. It became a zero-sum game.
The IRA said that giving up their weapons before being
invited to share power with the Unionists meant giving up
their trump card. The Unionists said they weren't going
into government with people who had a private army. Both
were reasonable positions, but the result was deadlock. So
what we had to do was ask questions. "What is it that *really*
matters to you?"'

It eventually became apparent that what the Unionists needed wasn't really decommissioning; after all, the
IRA could always get new weapons if they wanted them.
They needed the IRA to take the symbolic step of publicly
renouncing violence forever. As for the IRA themselves, they
had no intention of going back to violence. But they didn't
want to feel as if they were being forced into a surrender.
This conflict was at least as much about the intangibles of
face, pride and respect as it was about material goals.

Powell and Blair needed to find something that wasn't
quite decommissioning but that carried the necessary symbolic weight. 'The idea of weapons dumps came from
Kosovo and Bosnia. British generals told me that because
they couldn't get people to give up their weapons, they made
both sides' weapons available for inspection. So I went to a
house in West Belfast and met Gerry Adams and put this
to him. He said, 'There's absolutely *no way* we can accept
this'.' A month later, Adams returned to Powell with the
same proposal.

The symbolic step of burying weapons opened the way to a lasting peace deal. 'Terrorist groups don't want to be thought of as criminals, but as legitimate political movements,' Powell told me. Legitimacy, of course, being another word for respect.

One of America's most effective generals, Stanley McChrystal played key roles in the Iraq and Afghanistan wars, combining a reputation for ruthlessness in combat with a scholarly intellect. During an interview given after his retirement he summarised the difficult process of adaptation the US military went through in the years following the invasion of Baghdad – a process which led, eventually and belatedly, to a lasting reduction in violence:

When we first started, the question was, 'Where is the enemy?' That was the intelligence question. As we got smarter, we started to ask, 'Who is the enemy?' And we thought we were pretty clever. And then we realized that wasn't the right question, and we asked, 'What's the enemy doing or trying to do?' And it wasn't until we got further along that we said, 'Why are they the enemy?'

It has often been observed that the American military is obsessed with short-term results, and as a consequence can lose sight of longer-term goals. This is not a problem unique to the military, however. As a culture, we have a persistent tendency to pretend that asking 'what' can be substituted for 'why'. When we can, we avoid the murky waters of emotion and causation, and focus only on the measurable. Most economists work with a model of human behaviour that treats individuals as 'rational actors' who respond to incentives and disincentives but possess no deeper motivational complexity. Investors value companies according to their quarterly results rather than evaluating their long-term strategy.

For a good part of the twentieth century, even psychologists stopped asking *why* human beings behave in certain ways, and focused exclusively on what they *do*. Behaviourists, who dominated the field in the 1930s and 1940s, argued that it was futile to try and fathom people's inner feelings, thoughts or desires, and that the only proper object of study was the interplay between behaviour and environment, stimulus and response. Only with the arrival of the 'cognitive revolution' in the 1950s did it once again become acceptable to ask questions about motivation.

The familiar desire to do away with 'why' can be discerned underneath the contemporary enthusiasm for Big Data. The exponential increase in the processing power of computers, and the ubiquity of connected digital devices, mean there is more available information on human activity than ever before. Companies crunch data derived from our web and mobile phone use to work out what we're going to buy next. Social scientists, journalists and activists use similar techniques to map and predict the spread of disease, crime and famine.

The Failed State Index, for instance, is designed to be a scientific measure of which states around the world are close to collapse. Each country is rated on twelve indicators of 'pressure on the state' during the year in question – including refugee flows, poverty and security threats. The data is drawn from some 130,000 publically available sources. Its aim is to give 'an early warning of conflict . . . to policy-makers and the public at large.'

Chris Anderson, the former editor of *Wired* magazine, has made the extreme case for the potential of such techniques:

Out with every theory of human behavior, from linguistics to sociology. Forget taxonomy, ontology, and psychology. Who knows why people do what they do? The point is they do it, and we can track and measure it with unprecedented fidelity. With enough data, the numbers speak for themselves.

Anderson thinks that when you amass Big Data, you no longer have to bother with the Big Why. Every question should be treated as a puzzle rather than a mystery. But not everything is susceptible to such analysis. The Failed State Index failed utterly to predict the failure of Middle Eastern and North African states in early 2012 that became known as the Arab Spring. Only someone with a deep understanding of the relevant countries' politics and history would stand a chance of anticipating such events, analysing their causes or formulating a response.

As the authors of a more balanced assessment of Big Data put it, even as we make the most of its potential, 'There will be a special need to carve out a place for the human: to reserve space for intuition, common sense, and serendipity.' Knowing the 'what' is crucial to making good decisions and discoveries, but it will always be important to ask 'why'.

It's part of what makes us human, after all. When we stop asking why we become like Kanzi — intelligent apes who can monitor their environment, make requests and follow instructions, but who remain blind to deeper truths — like what my adversary is *really* asking of me.

5. BE A THINKERER

In 1773, on a wet and blustery October day, Benjamin Franklin led a group of men down to Portsmouth harbour on the south coast of England, where they boarded two boats and set out to sea. Franklin's boat put down anchor about a quarter of a mile from the shore. The other, at Franklin's instruction, pushed out a little further, and began to cross back and forth over the same stretch. As it did so, one of its passengers poured olive oil onto the waves out of a large stone bottle, through a hole in the cork 'somewhat bigger than a goose-quill'. The expedition's leader watched keenly from his small boat, as it pitched and tossed and the sea threw icy spray into his face.

Franklin was looking to see if the oil was flattening the surf. In his account of the expedition, he explained that his interest in the apparent capacity of oil to calm turbulent waters had first been aroused sixteen years before, when he was on his way to England on his first diplomatic mission as an emissary of the American colonies. Standing on deck, he noticed that the wake of his ship appeared remarkably smooth compared to that of the others in the fleet. He asked the ship's captain why this might be. The captain, with a hint of contempt for his question, replied that it was because the cooks had just emptied their greasy water through the scuppers.

In 1762, on a voyage from England to America, Franklin made himself a reading lamp by floating oil and a wick on some water in a glass which he hung from the ceiling of his cabin. He couldn't help but become more interested in what was happening inside his lamp than in his book. He noticed that when the ship rocked, the water in the lamp was 'in great commotion' but the oil remained in place, and that when the oil burned away to a thin film overnight the water stopped moving too.

Franklin asked a fellow passenger, a retired sea captain, for his thoughts. The old man said that the Bermudans used oil to smooth choppy waters, and that he had witnessed a similar practice in Lisbon. Another passenger with whom Franklin consulted recalled that divers in the Mediterranean would keep a small quantity of oil in their mouths as they descended into the deep and release it in order to smooth the waters above, thus allowing more light to reach down below.

Once ashore, Franklin described what he had observed to various of his learned friends, all of whom agreed it was interesting and, having promised to consider the matter, promptly forgot about it. Not Franklin. He couldn't forget about anything he couldn't explain. As one of his biographers puts it, Franklin 'could not drink a cup of tea without wondering why tea leaves gathered in one configuration rather than another at the bottom.'

A few years later Franklin, now back in England, could be found crouched at the edge of the large pond at Clapham Common, south of London. It was a windy day, and when he poured a little oil on the waves that spread from the side of the pond he saw that an instant calm was produced on the water, which spread until a quarter of the pond was 'as smooth as a looking glass.' After this, Franklin carried a vial of oil in the hollow of his bamboo walking stick everywhere he went, so that he could make similar experiments at every stream, pond or lake he passed on his walks.

Eventually, Franklin wondered if the wave-stilling effect would work reliably, not just on the gentle waves of a wind-disturbed pond, but on the high waves of an ocean swell, and if so whether it might be harnessed to help sailors land ashore in stormy waters. On the pond in London's Green Park, Franklin demonstrated his experiment to Count Bentinck of Holland and his son, a naval captain and amateur inventor. Captain Bentinck promptly invited Franklin to Portsmouth, where he provided him with the boats required for the larger-scale experiment Franklin had in mind, and accompanied him on the expedition.

Few questions escaped Franklin's penetrating curiosity. When he learned that the ocean voyage between England and America took two weeks longer going west than it did going east, he wondered if it was something to do with the rotation of the earth. But after a conversation with a Nantucket whaler, he discovered that a warm current of water was slowing down ships that travelled westward and speeding up those heading east. Franklin named it the Gulf Stream, and was the first to chart its course, by keeping track of the ocean's temperature during his Atlantic crossings. Every day he could be found on deck, taking daily temperature readings from the waters.

A portmanteau of 'think' and 'tinker', the origin of the verb 'to thinker' is unknown. I was introduced to it by Paola Antonelli of MoMA, who traced it to a presentation given in 2007 by John Seely Brown, a Silicon Valley legend and until 2000 a director of the legendary Xerox Palo Alto Research Centre (Xerox PARC). Brown and Antonelli use the term to describe a social, collaborative way of working. But I'm using it to name a style of cognitive investigation that mixes the concrete and the abstract, toggling between the details and the big picture, zooming out to see the wood and back in again to examine the bark on the tree. Here is Peter Thiel, venture capitalist and co-founder of PayPal, introducing a series of lectures he gave to students at Stanford University on the theme of entrepreneurialism:

> *A fundamental challenge – in business as in life – is to integrate the micro and macro such that all things make sense. Humanities majors may well learn a great deal about the world. But they don't really learn career skills through their studies. Engineering majors, conversely, learn in great technical detail. But they might not learn why, how, or where they should apply their skills in the workforce. The best students, workers, and thinkers will integrate these questions into a cohesive narrative.*

What Thiel describes here is what I'm calling thinkering. Benjamin Franklin was the archetypal thinkerer. Although undoubtedly an intellectual, he didn't fit the popular image of the philosopher, as captured by Auguste Rodin – a sedentary, solitary cogitator in repose, shuttered from the world's distractions. Franklin was a man of action, an implausibly productive doer who built better versions of things that already existed, like printing presses, and things that hadn't yet been born, like fire services and democratic republics. He was physically active (he once swam down the Thames from Chelsea to Westminster) and socially hyperactive; he loved to sit around a table with friends and new acquaintances, drinking coffee, telling stories, and making plans for a better world. He was as at home discussing airy abstractions like freedom and virtue as he was the best way to count a vote or to organise one's day, and he approached the former by way of the latter. Franklin loved *life*, with all of its surprises, kinks and uncertainties. His epistemic curiosity was fed by an accumulation of experiments, like what happens when you spread oil upon a pond. In the eighteenth century there were plenty of people who tinkered with Leyden jars but there were fewer with the intellectual toolkit to consider how the crackle in the jar related to the flashes in the sky.

In the 1990s the term 'symbolic analysts' was coined by the economist Robert Reich to describe the rise of jobs that use technology to shape, manipulate and sell units of significance rather than producing or moving physical goods. Symbolic analysts include those who work in marketing, software development and investing. They are PowerPoint wizards, who apply the same conceptual tools to every area of human endeavour; a management consultancy thinks about a company that makes TV programmes the same way it does a hospital that saves lives.

Reich was commentating on the shift in global economic activity that saw developing countries, most notably China, take over the bulk of the world's manufacturing, while Western countries became 'knowledge economies', exporting thoughts rather than goods. But the knowledge economy often seems to have little room for the kind of knowledge Franklin gained when he made himself a reading lamp. It is more interested in big ideas than physical process, and values conceptual breakthroughs over incremental progress. Meanwhile, the technical knowledge of the world is becoming increasingly specialised, the province of a few experts who find it hard to communicate what they know to those outside their own field and who, as Thiel suggests, find it hard to integrate their micro knowledge with the macro needs of the workplace and world.

Although he was writing three hundred years ago, David Hume saw that an economy needs a balance of thinkers and doers, and that each is improved by the other: 'The same age, which produces great philosophers and poets, usually abounds with skilful weavers, and ship-carpenters. We cannot reasonably expect, that a piece of woollen-cloth will be wrought to perfection in a nation, which is ignorant of astronomy, or where ethics are neglected.' Nor can we expect great ideas to flourish in a society, or a company, in which the details of craft are neglected. Here is Steve Jobs again, one of the heroes of the symbolic analyst class, and yet also a manufacturer:

You know, one of the things that really hurt Apple was after I left, John Sculley got a very serious disease. It's the disease of thinking that a really great idea is 90 per cent of the work. And if you just tell all these other people 'Here's this great idea', then of course they can go off and make it happen. And the problem with that is that there's just a tremendous amount of craftsmanship in between a great idea and a great product... Designing a product is keeping five thousand things in your brain and fitting them all together

in new and different ways to get what you want. And every
day you discover something new that is a new problem or a
new opportunity to fit these things together a little different.
And it's that process that is the magic.

Steve Jobs deserved the overused term 'visionary'. But he also, famously, obsessed over details; 323 Apple product patents list Steven P. Jobs as one of their inventors (they include one for the glass steps used in Apple stores). These two aspects of his outlook weren't contradictory; they depended on each other. Jobs was able to think differently about the future of personal computers, but only after he had spent time tinkering with the Apple Mac's forerunner, the Alto, at PARC. Jobs was a thinkerer.

The people responsible for our biggest ideas are usually detail freaks too. Open the pages of *The Origin of Species* for the first time and you discover a rather different book from the one you may have been led to expect. You will not find ringing declarations of intellectual revolution. What you will find are pages upon pages on the breeding of dogs and horses. Darwin's world-changing idea grows organically out of his empirical observation. Similarly, if you read Adam Smith's *The Wealth of Nations*, you find, before any mention of the invisible hand of the market, a closely observed account of the operations of a pin factory.

The experiment in Portsmouth harbour was a failure. While Franklin and his fellow investigators observed some smoothing of the waters around the boat, it had little effect on the height and force of the white-capped waves as they crested towards the coast and broke on the shore. But that was no matter to Franklin. He was careful to record the details 'even of an Experiment that does not succeed, since they may give Hints of Amendment in future Trials.' Indeed, Franklin's wave-stilling experiments took on a life beyond that of their instigator. As a recent paper in the *Biophysical Journal* attests, they inspired future scientists to investigate the action of molecule-thick layers ('monolayers') on water, and eventually to a better understanding of the properties of cell membranes, the semi-permeable wrappers that surround the basic building block of all living things.

We live in a very different world to Benjamin Franklin, one of far greater technological complexity, and as a consequence, greater abstraction. Most of us can't even begin to understand how the engine of a modern car functions, or how our smartphone works. Abstraction is the very principle on which the digital revolution is built – the world copied into zeroes and ones. The web allows us to skim and skip along the top line of everything, scooping out the gist without delving into details. Unless we make an effort to be thinkerers – to sweat the small stuff while thinking big, to get interested in processes *and* outcomes, tiny details *and* grand visions, we'll never recapture the spirit of the age of Franklin.

6. QUESTION YOUR TEASPOONS

On a freezing Sunday morning in the East End of London I took my place in a long line of people which disappeared around a distant corner. It was populated by the youthful inhabitants of one of London's hippest neighbourhoods, people not known for their eagerness to be up and about the morning after a Saturday night. They were wrapped in thick coats and wore woolly hats with ear-muffs. Gloved fingers slid across the screens of smartphones. The queue wasn't budging. I overheard someone say, 'We can hardly complain, can we? This is the Boring Conference.'

Eventually things got going, and we filed into a draughty Victorian building called York Hall, formerly renowned for its staging of boxing matches. Five hundred chairs in neat rows faced a stage, on which there was a podium and a big screen showing, in slow rotation, photographs of dull suburban streets. Overlaid on the pictures was a message, written in a stolid font: 'Welcome to Boring 2012. It won't be as good as last year.'

Despite this warning, excited chatter filled the hall. Now and again a cheer was heard; in one corner of the hall there was a competition to see who could make the most self-propelled rotations in an office chair from a single push. The people in the row behind me discussed the most efficient technique: 'Once you've achieved lift-off, you need to tuck your feet in and stick out your arms. It's the principle of conservation of momentum.'

James Ward, prime mover of the Boring conference, was first to speak. After a brief welcome consisting mainly of apologies he introduced his own Boring 2012 topic of choice – the history of supermarket self-checkout machines. Ward's presentation, entitled 'Unexpected Item in Bagging Area'*, was followed by a talk about letterboxes from someone who had spent time working as a postman. The challenge of 'protective bristles' was addressed.

Next, a stylishly dressed young woman called Leila Johnston told the audience about her obsession with IBM cash registers, as used in Starbucks and other retail chains. IBM's machines are, she asserted, superior to the Sharp or Toshiba alternatives. She showed photographs of different IBM models she had spotted while out shopping ('Now, here is something special: the EPOS 5600, *in white* – my Moby Dick.') together with a plot of their locations on a Google map. A man in a tight-fitting shirt talked about how to make perfectly browned 'hotel toast' at home. He started by explaining that he generally prefers to place the bread lengthways into the toaster, 'though obviously that depends on the aspect ratio of the bread.' The hall was cold, but it was warmed by the audience's evident pleasure in the

---

* Ward told us about how he once deliberately miscategorised portobello mushrooms as ordinary mushrooms, thus defrauding a supermarket of several pence. ('A security guard was standing right next to me as I carried out my mushroom hustle. I've never felt so alive.')

presentations. After a break for some ostentatiously boring refreshments (cucumber sandwiches), a music journalist gave a talk about double yellow lines.

Ward is a marketing manager by day, and co-founder of the Stationery Club, whose members convene to discuss pens, paper and paper clips. In 2010 he noted that a conference called 'Interesting' had just been cancelled. He took to Twitter to propose, half-jokingly, that it ought to be replaced with a Boring conference. To his surprise, the tweet provoked a wave of enthusiastic replies, including offers of contributions, ideas and assistance. So he asked a few people to prepare short presentations on a boring subject of their choice, booked a venue, and hoped that enough people would buy tickets to cover the deposit. The first fifty tickets sold in seven minutes, the rest soon followed.

The inaugural Boring conference was held in a room above the London theatre which houses a long-running musical based on the songs of the band Queen (the conference motto that year was 'We Will Not Rock You'). Ward kicked off proceedings of the first conference with a discussion of his tie collection, complete with PowerPoint charts (he noted, for example, that the proportion of single-colour ties in his collection fell from 45.5 per cent to 1.5 per cent between June and December that year). Ward's whimsical tweet had turned into a real world event that garnered national and international media coverage, including an article in the *Wall Street Journal*, anointing Ward the 'envoy of ennui'.

The conference has been repeated every year since, in a

succession of larger venues. It is dedicated to 'the mundane, the ordinary and the overlooked.' Over the years, topics have included electric hand dryers, paint catalogues, sneezing (the latter given by a man who had kept a diary of his sneezes for three years), car park roofs and bus routes. Beneath the dry irony and self-deprecating humour pervading the conference lies a serious purpose – to demonstrate that *anything* can be interesting.

The title of Ward's blog is borrowed from a saying of Andy Warhol's: 'I like boring things'. Warhol took the most boring and ubiquitous object he could think of – a tin of soup – and made millions of people see it anew. Ward says that when he refers to boring things he is thinking of things that only *seem* boring, because we're not paying attention to them. He quotes another avant-garde artist, the composer John Cage, 'If something is boring after two minutes, try it for four. If still boring, then eight. Then sixteen. Then thirty-two. Eventually one discovers that it is not boring at all.'

Ward calls this 'the transformative power of attention'. Car park roofs, hand dryers, milk; you can take anything, he says, and, by paying attention to it, reveal hidden interest, significance, beauty. Leila Johnston told the people in York Hall about how her childhood years were spent in a small town in Scotland, close to an IBM plant. The factory was the lifeblood of the town; the train station was named IBM Halt. Everyone's parents worked there, and children were used to playing with bags of IBM components as toys. Johnston explained that growing up like this not only made her forever interested in electronics, but left her with an abiding affection for Big Blue. Her audience was captivated. An apparently tedious topic had been transformed into a meaningful story about how we cherish our connections to childhood.

Ward is an admirer of the French writer Georges Perec, who was interested in the 'infra-ordinary', by which he meant the opposite of extraordinary: the background noise of life, the things we see or do every day. Our utensils, our habitual turns of phrase, are things so obvious and commonplace that we forget to see their inherent fascination. In an essay called *An Attempt at Exhausting a Place in Paris*, Perec takes a seat in the window of a café in Paris and describes everything he can see. Then he goes back the next day and does the same thing – and the next day, and the next. He wanted to find out 'what happens when nothing happens'. Perec urged his readers to 'question your teaspoons'.

Henry James was once accused by H.G. Wells of having sacrificed his life to art. He replied, 'I live, live intensely, and am fed by life, and my value, whatever it might be, is my own kind of expression of that. Art makes life, makes interest, makes importance.' When someone gets interested or bored we tend to praise or blame the object which interests or bores them. But some people are just better than others at 'making interest' in the world. It is a talent, or rather, an art. Henry James was fed by a life that was itself no more interesting than the lives most of us live – indeed, as Wells was suggesting, it was less interesting than many. But he turned his unpromising raw materials – observations made while walking in the park, gossip overheard at a dinner party – and transformed them into vividly imagined fictions.

James didn't feel a need to go chasing after experience, preferring to discover what was interesting in the experiences he had. His biographer Hazel Hutchinson told me that most of James's novels grew out of anecdotes told to him by friends, 'which he took away and chewed over, working out the reasons why the people involved behaved in the way that they did.' His advice to young writers was, 'Try to be one of the people upon whom nothing is lost!'

It is by studying little things that we attain the great art of having as little misery and as much happiness as possible
Samuel Johnson

Laura McInerney is a former teacher, now pursuing a PhD in education on a Fulbright scholarship. When she was an undergraduate she had a job at McDonald's. During the daily breakfast shift she would break and cook over 400 hundred eggs: 'Smash, crack, sizzle, remove. Repeat!' It was soul-destroying work, or at least, it might have been but for her capacity to get interested in what she was doing. She began getting interested in eggs and how they cook because of coagulation, a process that involves protein becoming so overwhelmed by heat that it ceases to be soluble and sets into a solid.

Suddenly, McInerney came to see each egg as a mini-battlefield, where proteins fought heat warriors. She started to watch each egg carefully to see which proteins gave up the ghost first – those in the middle or those at the edge. On other days, the eggs would remind her of a history class she took on Weimar Germany in which she learned that an egg went from costing a quarter of a Reichsmark to four billion Reichsmarks. Or she would reflect on eggs and morality – was it ethically right to steal eggs from a chicken? For McInerney, an egg wasn't just an egg.

When Carol Sansone was at university she found herself bored by the courses that she was taking, so she started to attend courses in things she was interested in, even though they didn't count towards her degree. In her mandated courses, she was the epitome of what educationalists call a 'surface learner'; she targeted her efforts efficiently, doing just what she needed to do to succeed. In courses she took for their own sake – an eclectic mix of art history, literature and creative writing – she was a 'deep learner', absorbed and enthralled by the material, seeking understanding for its own sake. Her tutors on these courses were pleased to have such an enthusiastic student in their class, but somewhat puzzled when she told them that she was gaining no credits from their course.

Sansone was puzzled too. She wondered why there seemed to be two distinct categories, not just in her life, but in the world – things you do because they're important, and things you do for pleasure. Or to put it another way, things you do to hit a target that others have set – a great degree, a top job – and things you do just because you are fascinated by the doing of them. Now, as a psychology professor at the University of Utah, she studies the strategies people use to make boring things interesting.

We have all found ourselves in situations where we're compelled – by our parents, our teachers, our bosses, our own conscience – to spend time on tasks that we find painfully dull. We can motivate ourselves to complete them by thinking about the money we'll get for doing it, or the approval of our teacher, or just the stuff we'll have to deal with if we don't do it. But we can also find ways to turn this mundane activity into something that stimulates our curiosity, knowing that once we get interested in it, we're more likely to spend time on it.

It's often assumed that motivating people involves getting them to think about the future – about what they can achieve or become. When head teachers, life coaches or personal trainers talk about motivation, they usually focus on the importance of *goals*. Work hard at this job, and you'll get promoted; to get through another set of bench presses, think about the kind of biceps you want. This makes sense – we all use the prospect of future benefits to drag ourselves through some tedious or unpleasant but necessary activity. But the goal-focused approach to motivation has its problems, because when we set our sights on the future we are less likely to enjoy the present, which can make what we're doing feel less interesting, and thus make us less likely to persevere with it.

Researchers from the University of Chicago and the Korea Business School collaborated on a study to investigate this phenomenon. They recruited a hundred students about to embark on a session at the gym. They asked half of them to describe their goals – 'I want to lose weight' – and then to continue focusing on those goals as they worked out. They asked the other half to describe their *experience* – what it was like stretching and exercising at the gym – and to continue thinking about that as they undertook their session.

Before the session, the goal-driven students tended to say they were planning to run on the treadmill for longer than the experience-focused students. But it was the experience-focused students who actually ended up running for longer, and who also reported enjoying their exercise more afterwards.* When all our interest is directed at the future, we get easily bored with the present. This puts a subtle twist on the classic distinction between intrinsic and extrinsic motivation. Extrinsic rewards aren't always offered or imposed upon us by a third party. We can set them ourselves, and in the process accidentally corrode our inner motivation.

If you are a manager or a teacher, then, is it best to encourage employees or students to explore their curiosity? Not if your overriding concern is that they perform a task

---

* For good measure, the researchers performed a similar experiment with people about to embark on classes or programmes of other activities, including origami, yoga and dental flossing. Similar results obtained (apparently it is possible to find even flossing interesting, if you try hard enough).

on time. As we've seen, getting interested in something means that future goals recede in importance. Sansone and her colleagues gave volunteers a repetitive word-copying task they spontaneously started to make it more interesting for themselves by varying the way they copied the letters and reading the incidental text. When they employed these interest-enhancing tricks, they copied fewer letters within the time allowed than they had before. However, when the time spent on the task was up to students, the ones who employed interest-enhancing strategies copied *more* letters, because they persisted for longer. Curiosity is likely to lead to better work, but only if it's allowed time to breathe.

It can lead to broader satisfactions too. If diversive curiosity is the flash and splash of novel stimuli, epistemic curiosity is a path you want to keep travelling down, even when the road is bumpy. Making such a journey can bring an important ancillary benefit. The English philosopher J.S. Mill argued that happiness is something that happens to us while we are pursuing some other purpose – that it approaches us sideways, 'like a crab'. His insight foreshadowed the research of Mihaly Csikszentmihalyi, the psychologist who coined the term 'flow' to describe the happiness that comes from being completely and unreflectively immersed in an activity, whether it's guitar playing, rock climbing, or studying molecular genetics. People who share something of Henry James's talent for getting interested in things – even things that might seem mundane –tend to be happier than those who don't.

This is true of couples as well as individuals. Arthur Aron is a psychologist at Stony Brook University in New York who specialises in the study of long-term romantic relationships. When he started getting interested in this area, he noted that there was a gap in the research. Most of it focused on conflict – why do couples argue? There were plenty of studies of jealousy, resentment and anxiety. A less dramatic and more common problem had been neglected – what happens when couples get bored?

Aron and his colleagues run a long-term study of married couples. Over a hundred couples from Michigan are interviewed about their relationships, individually and at home, at yearly intervals. Aron has gathered data on three specific questions, from the seventh and sixteenth years of marriage. First, 'During the past month, how often did you feel that your marriage was in a rut (or getting into a rut)?' Second, 'All in all, how satisfied are you with your marriage?' Thirdly, he looked at a visual measure of closeness in which participants were asked to select, from a series of circles overlapping to different degrees, 'the picture which best describes your marriage'.

Aron found that the couples who felt that their relationship had become a little boring after seven years of marriage experienced much lower satisfaction nine years later, irrespective of their levels of conflict and argument. Couples who felt unexcited by each other were also likely to choose pairs of circles that overlapped less with each other, to sum up their closeness. Boredom wasn't a neutral quality, a mere absence of excitement. It acted as a malign agent, quietly prising couples apart. In some ways it was more dangerous than open conflict. As Aron puts it, 'At least couples who argue with each other are still doing something together.'

Studies have shown that marital satisfaction tends to take a precipitous decline in the early years of the marriage. Part of the reason that couples drift apart from each other, Aron reasons, is that the novelty of mutual self-transformation wears off. It's thrilling to see the world through someone else's eyes; to feel your own being remoulded in response to another's. But when you're no longer getting to know each other's enthusiasms and quirks and unexpected strengths, when you've agreed on your favourite restaurants and holiday destinations, and got to know each others' friends, then it's time, according to Aron, to actively replenish the stock of novelty. The couples who do so are more likely to remain happy.

It's not enough to just order a new DVD box set, however; couples need to pursue activities which involve learning or achieving something together. In another study, Aron recruited twenty-eight couples from his university campus. Some were married, some dating for at least two months. They were taken to a gym hall and invited to take part in one of two different tasks. Some couples were given the 'mundane' task, which involved one partner rolling a ball to the centre of the room while the other watched, then retrieving the ball and rolling it back the other way. Others were given the 'novel and arousing' task, which involved being bound to each other with Velcro straps while negotiating an obstacle course. (Despite the faintly sadomasochistic flavour of the activity, the term 'arousing' here refers only to physiological and mental stimulation.)

The couples were then asked to fill out a questionnaire about their relationship, and some were filmed talking to each other, their conversation observed and coded according to established protocols for measuring the quality of marital interaction. The couples that engaged in the 'novel and arousing' activities were significantly more likely to express satisfaction in their relationship afterwards, and to feel romantically about the other. As Aron pointed out to me, couples who take part in such potentially awkward, embarrassing and frustrating experiences are more likely to fall out. But better that than being bored.

Aron doesn't prescribe a frantic search for utterly new experiences – 'We went paragliding last year, let's learn the Peruvian flute this summer' – so much as taking a gentle pleasure in variation, even if the themes are familiar. He told me that he and his wife (also a psychologist, and a collaborator) go hiking in the mountains of Slovenia, but always try different routes. Another researcher, James Graham of Western Washington University, found that happy couples were simply better at finding interest in the mundane joint activities of everyday life – cooking, childcare, DIY.

Henry James used curiosity to turn the ordinary stuff of life into great art. But then, he was a genius. The rest of us can, at the very least, use it to make our lives more interesting. It's a choice: we can interrogate our cutlery, or allow the familiar to be boring. Laura McInerney expresses the principle beautifully:

> When you live somewhere boring — and we *all* live somewhere boring — then we have a choice about the way we will see that place. We can spend our days thinking like everyone else, seeing the same things over and over, and never once wondering about how they got that way, or why they stayed that way, or how they could be better. Or, we can learn. And if we make the choice to learn, and to be *curious* about the things around us, then we are essentially making the choice never to be bored again.

7. TURN PUZZLES INTO MYSTERIES

In 1955, a bow-tied man with silver hair and a fastidiously trimmed moustache cleared his belongings from a government office in Washington. William Friedman was retiring from his post at the US National Security Agency, bringing an end to a world-changing career very few people knew about.

He took with him a photograph he had kept under the glass plate that covered his desk. It heads this section. In it, seventy-one uniformed officers stand in two lines behind a seated row of five men and women in civilian clothes. At first glance the image is unremarkable, but a second look reveals something odd about the way the subjects are posed. Some face the front but have their head turned to the right, some are square to the camera, others have their whole bodies facing one way or the other.

For more than thirty years, Friedman was the US government's chief code-breaker. He was the leader of the team that broke Japan's 'Purple' cipher – equivalent to the German Enigma machine – thus providing the US government with vital intelligence on Japanese activities during the war, including information that, had it been acted on, might have averted Pearl Harbor. He was also co-inventor of the US army's best cipher machine, and is regarded as one of the founders of the modern study of cryptography. In this book I've talked about the difference in curiosity about puzzles and mysteries. Friedman's expertise was literally in puzzles, but he exemplifies the ability of the curious mind to find fulfilment in pursuing the insoluble.

Friedman's hero was the great Renaissance scholar and statesman Sir Francis Bacon, and it was from Bacon that Friedman took his fascination with codes. Bacon invented a code called the 'bilateral cipher', in which a combination of only two symbols is used, in groups of five, to represent every letter in the alphabet. So, for instance, if the two symbols are *a* and *b*, A = *aaaaa*, B = *aaaab*, C = *aaaba*, and so on. The crucial point in Bacon's system is that rather than using *a*'s and *b*'s (which would make the code relatively easy to decipher) he proposed using anything that can be divided into two classes or types: two types of font, bells and trumpets, apples and oranges. As Bacon put it, such a system enabled people to say 'anything by means of anything'.

Bacon's system was never used, as he had thought it would be, to transmit military secrets, but it became a tool used by literary sleuths. From the latter half of the nineteenth century onwards, many learned people became convinced that Shakespeare was not the author of his plays, and that the answer to the question of who was could be found in puzzles buried within the texts.* Sir Francis Bacon was a leading candidate, and 'Baconians' believed his bilateral cipher offered the key to the answer. One of the men most interested in this question was the eccentric American millionaire George Fabyan, heir to the country's largest cotton goods firm. He lured Elizabeth Gallup, author of a highly successful book of Baconian investigation, to come and work on 'the Greatest of Literary problems' at his estate at Riverbank, on the Fox river, just west of Chicago. Gallup was

---

* The Shakespeare conspiracy theorists included Henry James, Mark Twain and Sigmund Freud, proving that very smart people can believe very silly things.

joining an avant-garde faculty of scientists at Riverbank, dedicated, as Fabyan put it, to 'wresting from Nature, her secrets'.

Fabyan had the main building redesigned by Frank Lloyd Wright and added a Japanese garden, a lighthouse, a zoo (with a gorilla named Hamlet) and a Dutch windmill, moved brick by brick from Holland. In these bizarre surroundings, a diverse group of scientists were paid to pursue their own obsessions. In 1915, William Friedman joined them, after Fabyan persuaded him to leave his PhD in plant biology at Cornell to work at Riverbank on the propagation of wheat. Friedman's fascination with codes and bibliography meant that he soon joined Elizabeth Gallup's Department of Ciphers.

Before long, Friedman lost faith in the methods and purpose of Gallup's project (much later, he co-authored a book that demolished the arguments of Gallup and other Baconians). But it was at Riverbank that he developed his curiosity about codes into a fascination by which he would be happily consumed for the rest of his life. He created ever more elaborate cryptological designs, including a card he used for correspondence featuring a botanical plant, in which, to the initiated, everything – the roots, the leaves, the veins in the leaves – is a cipher (the roots spell out 'Bacon', the flower spells 'Shakespeare', while the leaves contain the names of other Elizabethan authors).

Another of Friedman's designs was of a page of sheet music for Stephen Foster's popular nineteenth-century song

'My Old Kentucky Home, Good Night,' that on *much* closer examination (some of the notes have small gaps in them, and some are whole, thus becoming *a*-types and *b*-types) reveals a secret message: 'Enemy advancing right/we march at daybreak.' At the bottom Friedman writes (in plain text): 'An example of making anything signify anything.'

A puzzle is something that commands our curiosity until we have solved it. A mystery, by contrast, never stops inviting enquiry. When we first meet a new problem, our instinct is to treat it as a puzzle: What's the answer? Then, after gathering the knowledge we need to solve it, we sometimes start to think of the same problem as a mystery, one which will sustain our curiosity forever. A passing interest can be transformed into a lifelong passion.

When we come across a puzzle of any kind, we should always be alert to the mystery that lies behind it, because it might be a mystery that that will occupy and entertain us long after the puzzle is solved. William Friedman loved puzzles, in the most literal sense of that word. But his curiosity about them went far beyond any single example. At Riverbank, he came to think of the most fundamental principle of cryptology – that 'anything can signify anything' – as an inexhaustible mystery, in which he took a profound and enduring delight. Puzzles are stepping stones to mysteries. The more mysteries we pursue, the more knowledge we gather, the greater our intellectual and cultural range.

During the First World War, the US government, hearing of Friedman's work at Riverbank, called on him to train army units in cryptography. After doing so, Friedman joined the army himself. On returning from France, he went back to work at Riverbank for a few more years before moving to Washington with his wife (one of Elizabeth Gallup's assistants). Both put their cryptographic skills to work for the American government. Following his heroic efforts in cracking Japanese codes, Friedman rose to become chief cryptologist for the National Security Agency (NSA). He left behind a body of work that defined his field of study for decades afterwards.

Friedman liked to remind people that meaning can reside in the most unlikely places. The photograph on his desk was taken in Aurora, Illinois, on a winter's day in 1918, at the training school where he and his wife taught cryptography to army officers about to be sent to France. What did Friedman see when he looked at it? He saw his younger self seated at one end of the front row, facing inwards. He saw his wife in the middle, and at the other end, the imposing figure of George Fabyan. He also saw a message, hiding in plain sight. The image is a cryptogram in which people stand in for letters. Thanks to Friedman's careful positioning, the soldiers spell out Sir Francis Bacon's most famous axiom: 'KNOWLEDGE IS POWER.'

AFTERWORD
Bjarni

The first European to land in North America was not Christopher Columbus, but a Norse explorer named Leif Eriksson. According to Nordic saga – recently supported by archaeological evidence – Eriksson established a settlement at a place he called Vinland, on what is now the northern tip of Newfoundland, in modern-day Canada.

In the sagas, there are two conflicting accounts of how he got there. One is that, early in the third millennium, Eriksson was blown off course during a voyage from Norway to Greenland, where he aimed to convert the locals to Christianity. Another gives him more credit, suggesting that he set out from Norway fully intending to visit the New World, after hearing about it from another sailor. If the latter version is true, Eriksson was the first European to land in the New World, but he wasn't the first to *see* it. That honour goes to the guy who tipped him off: Bjarni Herjolfsson.

Born and raised in Iceland, Bjarni was a merchant captain based in Norway. In about AD 986, he made his annual summer voyage home to see his parents. He arrived at the end of his journey only to find that his father wasn't home, having gone on a journey to Greenland with Eric the Red* (the sagas do not record how Bjarni felt about this).

A dutiful son, Bjarni and his crew set sail for Greenland. On the way, they encountered a great storm that lasted for several days, and their small ship was blown many miles off course. When the storm cleared, Bjarni and the crew could see land. It looked nothing like the glacial and inhospitable Greenland, however. This land was covered in dense forests and rolling green hills. Bjarni's crew, intrigued by the prospect of an earthly paradise, begged their captain to allow them to go ashore. But Bjarni refused. He had a mission – to find his father – and he wasn't about to be diverted from it. He ordered the crew to head north. America remained undiscovered.

Even in his own day Bjarni was criticised for not seizing the opportunity with which fate had presented him. But let's try, for a moment, to see things from his point of view. Bjarni was a merchant, and a son, and he wanted to get to Greenland before the onset of winter so that he could settle there with his family, and trade his cargo. A trip to see an unknown land must have seemed like an unnecessary and dangerous distraction.

Curiosity is all very well in hindsight. But when it's happening, it drags us away from our tasks and our goals,

* Leif Eriksson's father, and the founder of Greenland.

bending our days out of shape. Like the narrator of Robert Frost's 'Stopping by Woods on a Snowy Evening', when we are in the grip of curiosity we easily forget about what we're supposed to be doing and become absorbed by the mystery of falling snow. These days we correctly regard the pre-modern prohibition of curiosity as repressive and archaic. But Augustine and others were right, in a sense – curiosity *is* a kind of perversion, a swerving away or deviation from the task at hand. Fabyan's project at Riverbank was at once admirable and slightly mad, a rich man's indulgence. Bjarni's men wanted to explore the verdant land they saw, no doubt dreaming of untold riches and willing virgins. But Bjarni had promises to keep.

Curiosity's difficulties are worthwhile, however. In a speech to Kenyon College's graduating class of 2005 the novelist David Foster Wallace made the case that the practice of curiosity is vital to a happy and well-lived life. His premise was that we are all, inevitably, helplessly self-centred:

> *Think about it: there is no experience you have had that you are not the absolute centre of. The world as you experience it is there in front of YOU or behind YOU, to the left or right of YOU, on YOUR TV or YOUR monitor. Other people's thoughts and feelings have to be communicated to you somehow, but your own are so immediate, urgent, real.*

It's only through the exercise of our curiosity about others, suggested Wallace, that we can free ourselves from our hard-wired self-obsession. We should do this, not just because it is the virtuous thing to do, but because it's the best way to cope with the 'boredom, routine and petty frustration' of everyday life. He gives the examples of standing in a long line at the supermarket checkout or getting caught in an end-of-day traffic jam. Tired and hungry, you can become furious at everyone around you and bemoan your own singular agony, or, 'if you're aware enough to give yourself a choice,' you can choose to look differently at the scene in which you find yourself. Imagine that the woman screaming at her kid in the checkout line has been up for three nights in a row nursing her sick husband, or that the driver who just cut you off is trying to get his child to hospital.

This, submits Wallace, is the purpose of education – 'the job of a lifetime'. Being educated involves understanding how to think, and thus escape our default setting. I think this is wise and true. Where I think Wallace goes wrong is when he says that this ability has 'almost nothing to do with knowledge'. It has everything to do with knowledge. Firstly, even empathic curiosity depends on epistemic curiosity; putting yourself in the shoes of the woman in the supermarket line requires a little knowledge of what it's like to live a life far removed from one's own. Secondly, as we've seen, thinking skills don't exist separately from knowledge, but grow out of it. Thirdly, worldly knowledge offers you another escape route from self-obsession; in the traffic jam, you could think about the book you read recently on the history of Roman Britain, as Laura McInerney considered the chemistry of eggs.

The writer Geoff Dyer describes depression, from which he has suffered, as 'the complete absence of any interest in anything.' In his book *Out of Sheer Rage*, Dyer describes how, when he was depressed, he went from being someone who was voraciously interested in the world – who read and travelled incessantly and widely – to someone who couldn't think of a single thing that he wanted to do, see or read. 'I had no interest in anything, no curiosity.' He spent his days in his apartment, watching a TV that wasn't turned on.

Eventually, a switch inside him flipped: Dyer became interested in his own mental condition. He read William Styron's memoir of depression, *Darkness Visible*, and Julia Kristeva's discussion of melancholia, *Black Sun*. In the latter, he came across a passage from Dostoevsky on Holbein's *Dead Christ*, which reactivated a long-dormant interest Dyer had had in the ways writers write about paintings. He started to think about the museums and exhibitions he would like to visit. Before he knew it, 'I was interested in the world again.' The psychoanalyst and writer Adam Phillips has said that he sees his purpose as a therapist being, somewhat paradoxically, 'to free people not to have to bother to be interested in themselves.' Happiness, he believes, is associated with the realisation that 'the only interesting things are outside oneself.'

The popular American comic book writer Matt Fraction received a harrowingly honest note on his website from a fan who revealed that he or she was contemplating suicide, saying, 'I know there is beauty and wonderful things in this world ... But what if I'm not interested?' In Fraction's reply, worth reading in full (I provide a link in the endnotes), he recalled a time when he himself had felt very close to suicide, and what it was that got him through:

> I wondered, then – well, is there anything you're curious about. Anything you want to see play out. And i thought of a comic i was reading and i'd not figured out the end of the current storyline. And i realized I had curiosity. And that was the hook i'd hang my hat on. that by wanting to see how something played out I wasn't really ready. That little sprout of a thing poking up through all that black earth kept me around a little longer.

Curiosity is a life force. If depression involves a turning inwards, a feeling that there's nothing in the world that is worthy of our attention (or that nothing we pay attention to is worthy) then it is curiosity which takes us the other way, that reminds us that the world is an inexhaustibly diverting, inspiring, fascinating place. It's a sentiment beautifully expressed in this passage from *The Once and Future King*, by T.H. White:

> The best thing for being sad,' replied Merlin, beginning to puff and blow, 'is to learn something. That's the only thing that never fails. You may grow old and trembling in your

anatomies, you may lie awake at night listening to the dis-
order of your veins, you may miss your only love, you may
see the world about you devastated by evil lunatics, or know
your honour trampled in the sewers of baser minds. There
is only one thing for it then – to learn. Learn why the world
wags and what wags it. That is the only thing which the mind
can never exhaust, never alienate, never be tortured by, never
fear or distrust, and never dream of regretting. Learning is
the only thing for you. Look what a lot of things there are
to learn.

Today, our capacity to absorb information is hopelessly over-matched by the amount of information worth learning. I can sympathise with the fear David Foster Wallace expressed as one of drowning in 'Total Noise', 'the Tsunami of available fact, context and perspective'. But any reservations I have about our contemporary cognitive environment pale in comparison to my overwhelming feelings of gratitude. I feel lucky to be living in an age when our collective memory wells are so deep. We have never known more than we do today about why the world wags and what wags it.

Isaac Newton, writing in 1676, felt he was standing on the shoulders of giants. From our own heady vantage point, early in the second millennium, we can take in a view of breathtaking majesty; a better one than was available to Newton, or to Thomas Jefferson or Albert Einstein, not to mention the billions of ordinary men and women who preceded us, most of whom, no matter how naturally curious, were confined to intellectual universes tiny compared to our own. Not only is there more knowledge, there's more access to it; unlike nearly everyone who have ever lived, if you want to learn about Montaigne, or genetic science, or black holes, or modernist architecture or the theories of Friedrich Hayek, you can. The same is true of cultural knowledge; it's an obvious but easily forgotten truth that it is better to have lived after Beethoven, and after The Beatles, than before them.

So will you take advantage of this sublimely lucky break or not?

Epistemic curiosity can be tough to justify in the moment. It is hard work, it diverts us from our tasks and goals, and we never quite know where it will take us. But we have a choice. We can decide to explore the worlds of knowledge that present themselves to us. Or, like Bjarni, we can turn our face from the beauty and the mystery and make for the next appointment.

ACKNOWLEDGEMENTS

I owe a great debt to the experts who took the time to talk to me, and to friends and acquaintances who helped out with indispensable ideas, insights and encouragement. They include Daron Acemoglu, Paola Antonelli, Art Aron, David Bain, Katarina Begus, Colin Campbell, Chris Cook, David Dobbs, David Dwan, Cora Dzubak, Susan Engel, Amanda Feve, Teodora Gliga, Hazel Hutchinson, Sean Holden, Maira Kalman, Annette Lareau, Linsey McGoey, Janet Metcalfe, Jonathan Powell, Mikkel Ramussen, Violet Rosser, Dan Rothstein, Carol Sansone, Brian Smith, Sophie von Stumm, Rory Sutherland, Daniel Willingham and Jack Woodward. I'd like to thank John Lloyd in particular for being so generous with his time and wisdom.

Thanks also to those who have helped me unwittingly, including the many experts to whom I didn't get to talk, but whose ideas and research inform this book. Annie Murphy Paul's education newsletter has been a constant source of inspiration and information, as has Tyler Cowen's blog *Marginal Revolution*. I have also been stimulated and sustained by *The Browser*, *Brain Pickings*, the *Radiolab* podcasts, and too many of those I follow on Twitter to mention. As I say, the internet *can* be a superb instrument of curiosity.

Thank you to my wonderful agent, Nicola Barr, whose enthusiasm kept this book afloat when its author's motivation was in the doldrums. Thanks to my US agent Celeste Fine for believing that this book deserved an American readership. Thank you to Quercus and all who sail in her, particularly my editor Richard Milner, and to Basic Books, especially Tisse Takagi. I'm grateful to Stephen Brown for his comments on the first chapters. Thanks to the staff at the Wellcome Library. Thank you to my mother, Margaret Leslie, and my brother, Stephen Leslie, for their encouragement and suggestions. My father passed away during the writing of this book; otherwise, I would be thanking him for instilling in me, by example, both epistemic and empathic curiosity. Lastly, thank you to my wife Alice, my best editor, best friend and amazing mother to our inveterately curious daughter.

Notes

I cite most of my sources in the text; here I attempt to give a bit more context where necessary and guide the reader in search of further reading.

INTRODUCTION
The Fourth Drive

I first read about Kanzi in Professor Paul Harris's fascinating book, *Trusting What You're Told: How Children Learn from Others*. It was Harris who made the point that despite Kanzi's exceptional intelligence, he displays no evidence of intellectual curiosity. John Lloyd was kind enough to share his insights into the nature of curiosity during a memorable interview at the *QI* offices in central London. Sophie von Stumm, one of our foremost researchers into curiosity, introduced me to the concept of 'need for cognition'. I came across the da Vinci notebook fragments via the blog of Robert Krulwich, with whom I'm familiar from *Radiolab*, a regular and delicious source of epistemic stimulation. The work of the psychologist Paul Silvia on the nature of 'interest' was influential on my early thinking. George Loewenstein's comprehensive and lucid account of the history of research into curiosity, which culminates in his proposal of a new theory, was invaluable, and where I first read about the distinction between diversive and epistemic curiosity. The statistic about average shot times in American movies is from an article in the *Wall Street Journal* by Rachel Dodes, who cites John Belton of Rutgers University. I owe Annie Murphy Paul for my discovery of Robert Wilson's extraordinary study of ageing brains. The Charles Eames quote I first came across on Maria Popova's indispensable blog *Brain Pickings*.

CHAPTER ONE
Three Journeys

When I came across Brian Smith's account of his childhood encounter with a gun I knew I wanted to use it for this book. I thank him for consenting to me doing so. Alexander Arguelles tells his own story as well as you would expect on his website, and is interviewed in *Mezzofanti's Gift*, Michael Erard's book about extraordinary language learners. David Dwan, author of *The Cambridge Companion to Edmund Burke*, was kind enough to discuss Burke with me. Stephen Kaplan's essay on the evolutionary origins of curiosity introduced me to the research on art and mystery. The neuroscience research I describe was led by Colin Camerer at Caltech. Mark Pagel's book about the human facility for cooperation, *Wired for Culture*, was influential on my thinking about what curiosity is for.

CHAPTER TWO
How Curiosity Begins

I spent a fascinating day at Babylab and I am very grateful to Teodora and Katarina for being so generous with their time and expertise. My daughter Io wasn't yet born when I visited but she has since been to Babylab as a research subject, and wears an EEG cap with panache. Alison Gopnik, as well as being an eminent psychologist, is a terrific writer, and I have absorbed much of what I know about early childhood development from her pieces, starting with the book she co-wrote with Andrew Meltzoff and Patricia Kuhl, *The Scientist in the Crib*. The longitudinal study of early exploratory behaviour and adolescent achievement was authored by Marcus Bornstein and colleagues (see bibliography). I came across Michelle Chouinard's research, and much more about the history of research into question-asking, in Paul Harris's book. I am grateful to my friends with young children for providing me with examples of their questions.

CHAPTER THREE
Puzzles and Mysteries

Susan Engel was very generous with her time and expertise on curiosity in childhood. I first came across the distinction between exploring and exploiting in Alison Gopnik's work. George Loewenstein's review of curiosity research, already mentioned, informed my account of theories of curiosity. I am grateful to Janet Metcalfe for helping me understand the significance of Daniel Berlyne's work. I found da Vinci's description of being at the entrance to a cave in an essay by Hans Blumenberg, one of the great historians of curiosity. Ben Greenman's article about his son was formative in my thinking about the relationship between curiosity and the internet.

CHAPTER FOUR
Three Ages of Curiosity

A key source for my discussion of the history of curiosity in Western society was *Curiosity and Wonder from the Renaissance to the Enlightenment*, a collection of essays edited by Evans and Marr. My discussion of curiosity cabinets was partly inspired by a wonderful illustrated blog post on the subject by the historian Benjamin Breen. My description of the key figures of Britain's 'Industrial Enlightenment' is coloured by Jenny Uglow's excellent book, *The Lunar Men*, and my conception of it as a grassroots revolution in curiosity was influenced by Roy Porter's work. It was Ethan Zuckerman who directed me to the origin of the term serendipity. I first came across Vannevar Bush's essay via *Brain Pickings*.

CHAPTER FIVE
Curiosity's Rising Rewards

I first came across the concept of the 'new' digital divide in an article in the *New York Times* by Matt Richtel. Pew Research carries out regular research into various aspects of the 'digital divide', as does the Kaiser Family Foundation. Richtel also authored a piece for *The Times* on technology and teaching, which mentions the 'Wikipedia problem'.

CHAPTER SIX
The Power of Questions

I spent a fascinating hour on the phone with Dan Rothstein; you can read more about his foundation's work and techniques in his book *Make Just One Change*. The research into question-asking I cite is drawn from Paul Harris's review of it in his book, *Trusting What You're Told*. Annette Lareau's book, *Unequal Childhoods*, is a great work of observational sociology and an engrossing read. I came across the case of Jerome Keviel via Linsey McGoey's work.

CHAPTER SEVEN
The Importance of Knowing

I am deeply influenced in my thinking about education by the work of Daniel Willingham, who provides a lucid, reasonable, evidence-based voice in a field full of sound and fury. I recommend his book, *Why Don't Students Like School?* I'm also indebted to Daisy Christodoulou's deeply researched and powerfully argued book, *Seven Myths about Education*, which everyone interested in the subject should read. Richard Mayer's work is cited in an excellent paper by Richard Clark and colleagues on the weight of evidence for 'fully guided instruction'. The quote from a teaching union is from an unsigned piece on the website of the Association of Teachers and Lecturers: 'A 21st-century curriculum cannot have the transfer of knowledge at its core for the simple reason that the selection of what is required has become problematic in an information-rich age.' It's a statement that is depressing in more than one way, one of them being the implication that if something is problematic you should give up on it.

CHAPTER EIGHT
Seven Ways to Stay Curious

1. STAY FOOLISH

The definitive biographies of Walt Disney and Steve Jobs are by, respectively, Neal Gabler and Walter Isaacson. The details on Jeff Bezos are drawn from a profile by Peter Whoriskey in the *Washington Post*, published shortly after Bezos became its owner.

2. BUILD THE DATABASE

Young's book on idea production is still in print; I urge you to obtain a copy and start producing.

3. FORAGE LIKE A FOXHOG

I am very grateful to the brilliant Paola Antonelli for taking the time to talk to me. Our conversation helped me form my thinking on the links between curiosity and creativity. Charlie Munger's 'Lesson on Elementary, Worldly Wisdom . . .' is available on the web. For a superb exposition of the value of being a generalist, read Robert Twigger's essay for *Aeon*, entitled 'Master of Many Trades', available online.

4. ASK THE BIG WHY

I'm grateful to Jonathan Powell for telling me as much as he was able to about his extraordinary work. His book about the Northern Ireland peace process, *Great Hatred, Little Room*, offers a revealing insight into the intense, relentless and often futile-seeming negotiations that eventually led to a lasting settlement.

5. BE A THINKERER

Benjamin Franklin's commitment to epistemic curiosity was at once admirable and slightly chilling. In his autobiography he relates how, on a return to Boston after many years away, he visited the boarding house run by his mother, whom he hadn't seen since he was a child. Instead of immediately reintroducing himself to her, he spent an evening observing her as if he was just another guest, interested to see whether some maternal intuition would enable her to recognise him. I was alerted to Franklin's interest in the effect of oil on water by Edmund Morgan's superb biography of Franklin. I found more details, including the trip to Portsmouth harbour, in Charles Tanford's book. I am grateful to Mikkel Ramussen, an innovation specialist at the ReD consultancy in Denmark, for the point about the importance of details to big thinking, which emerged over the course of a fascinating and fruitful conversation in London.

6. QUESTION YOUR TEASPOONS

James Ward's blog, *I Like Boring Things*, is a good resource for those interested in the same, and contains details of upcoming Boring conferences. George Perec was a minor genius of twentieth-century literature; his idiosyncratic, profoundly intelligent fiction and essays are worth investigating if you haven't already. Hazel Hutchinson, who has written an excellent short biography of Henry James, kindly took the time to help me understand the nature and uses of The Master's curiosity. Laura McInerney keeps an excellent blog about education. I'm grateful to Carol Sansone for talking to me and pleased that she has found work that is both interesting and important. Arthur Aron was also generous with his time and insights.

7. TURN PUZZLES INTO MYSTERIES

My account of William Friedman's career draws from a superb essay in *Cabinet* magazine by William H. Sherman. Readers can consult the article online for a fuller account, including more details on messages hidden in that photograph. Friedman didn't quite succeed in spelling out 'KNOWLEDGE IS POWER': they were four people short of the number needed to complete the 'R'. Friedman, who is buried in Arlington National Cemetery, had the same phrase inscribed as his epitaph.

AFTERWORD
Bjani

Matt Fraction's stirring reply to his depressed correspondent can be found here http://mattfraction.com/post/63999786236/ sorry-to-put-this-on-you-but-i-have-an-honest-question

Bibliography

ABC News, *Kids Have Fatal Attraction To Guns*, 9 August 2009.

Abrams, J.J., 'The Magic of Mystery', *Wired* magazine, 20 April 2009.

Arguelles, Alexander, 'Education and Experience', at Arguelles' personal website www.foreignlanguageexpertise.com

Aron, A., Strong, G., and Fincham, F., 'When Nothing Bad Happens But You're Still Unhappy; Boredom in Romantic Relationships', *The Inquisitive Mind*, 2012, Issue 13.

Atran, Scott and Ginges, Jeremy, 'How Words Could End a War', *New York Times*, 24 January 2009.

Begus, Katarina, and Southgate, Victoria, 'Infant Pointing Serves an Interrogative Function', *Developmental Science*, 2012, pp. 1–8.

Begus, Katarina, Gliga, Teodora, and Southgate, Victoria, 'Increase in Theta Band Activation in Expectation of Novel Information', in press, 2013.

Begus, Katarina, Gliga, Teodora, and Southgate, Victoria,

'Pointing Signals Infants' Readiness to Learn', in press, 2013.

Bell, Silvia, and Salter Ainsworth, Mary D., 'Attachment, Exploration and Separation: Illustrated by the Behaviour of One Year Olds in a Strange Situation', *Child Development*, Vol. 41, March 1970.

Berlin, Isaiah, *The Hedgehog and The Fox*, Phoenix, 1992.

Blumenberg, Hans, *The Legitimacy of the Modern Age*, in Evans and Marr, 2006.

Bornstein, Marcus, Hahn, Chun-Shin, and Sulwalsky, Joan T.D., 'Physically Developed and Exploratory Young Infants Contribute to Their Own Long-Term Academic Achievement', *Psychological Science*, August 2013.

Breen, Benjamin, 'Cabinets of Curiosity, The Web as Wunderkammer', http://theappendix.net/ blog/2012/11/cabinets-of-curiosity:-the-web-as-wunderkammer

Buss, Arnold, 'Evolutionary Perspectives on Personality Traits', in Hogan, Robert (ed.), *Handbook of Personality Psychology*, Academic Press, 1997.

Camerer, Colin et al., 'The Wick in the Candle of Learning: Epistemic Curiosity Activates Reward Circuitry and Enhances Memory', *Psychological Science*, November 2008.

Cacioppo, John T., Petty, Richard E., Feinstein, Jeffrey A., Jarvis, W. and Blair G., 'Dispositional Differences in Cognitive Motivation: The Life and Times of Individuals Varying in Need for Cognition', *Psychological Bulletin*, 1996, Vol. 119, No. 2, pp. 197–253.

Bibliography

Cacioppo, John T., Petty, Richard E., and Kao, Chuan Feng,
　　'The Efficient Assessment of Need for Cognition', *Journal
　　of Personality Assessment*, 1984, Vol. 48, No. 3.

Cai, Denise et al., 'REM, Not Incubation, Improves Creativity
　　by Priming Associative Networks', *PNAS*, June 2009.

Chuan, Tan Chorh, '10 Questions: Shaping Curious Minds',
　　Singapore Magazine, July 2013.

Christensen, Clayton, *The Innovator's Dilemma*, Harvard
　　Business Review Press, 2013.

Christodoulou, Daisy, *Seven Myths about Education*, Routledge,
　　2014.

Churchill, Winston, *A Roving Commission: My Early Life*,
　　C. Scribner's Sons, 1939.

Clark, Richard, Kirschner, Paul A., and Sweller, John, 'Putting
　　Students on the Path to Learning: The Case for Fully
　　Guided Instruction', *American Educator*, Spring 2012.

Comer-Kidd, David, and Castano, Emanuele, 'Reading
　　Literary Fiction Improves Theory of Mind', *Science*,
　　3 October 2013.

Cowen, Tyler, *The Great Stagnation*, Penguin/Dutton, 2012.

Cowen, Tyler, *Average Is Over*, Dutton, 2013.

Cowen, Tyler, interview with Eric Barker, http://www.
　　bakadesuyo.com/2013/09/average-is-over/

Cskiszentmihalyi, Mihaly, *Creativity*, Harper Collins, 1996.

Daston, Lorraine and Park, Katharine, *Wonders and the Order
　　of Nature, 1150-1750*, Zone Books, 1998.

Darwin, Charles, letter to J.D. Hooker, 11 January 1844.
　　http://www.darwinproject.ac.uk/entry-729

Dewey, John, *Interest and Effort in Education*, Houghton Mifflin, 1913.

Dodes, Rachel, 'Lingering Shots in an Age of Quick Cuts', *Wall Street Journal*, 21 February 2013.

Dolby, Ray, quoted in the *New York Times*, via Associated Press, 'Founder of Dolby Laboratories Dies', 12 September 2013.

Dwan, David, *Cambridge Companion to Edmund Burke*, Cambridge University Press, 2012.

Dylan, Bob, *Chronicles, Volume One*, Pocket Books, 2004.

Elliot, Jane, and Rhodes, John David, "The Value of Frustration": An Interview with Adam Phillips.' *World Picture Journal*, No. 7, 2012.

Engel, Susan, and Levin, Sam, 'Harry's Curiosity', in *The Psychology of Harry Potter*, Neil Mulholland (ed.), Smart Pop, 2007.

Erard, Michael, *Mezzofanti's Gift*, Duckworth Overlook, 2013.

Evans, James, 'Electronic Publishing and the Narrowing of Science and Scholarship', *Science*, 18 July 2008.

Evans, R.J.W, and Marr, Alexander (eds.), *Curiosity and Wonder from the Renaissance to the Enlightenment*, Ashgate, 2006.

Fallows, James, 'Blind into Baghdad', *Atlantic*, January 2004.

Ferreira, Fernando and Waldfogel, Joel, 'Pop Internationalism: Has Half a Century of World Music Displaced Local Culture?', *National Bureau of Economic Research*, May 2010.

Feynman, Michelle (ed.), *Perfectly Reasonable Deviations from the Beaten Track: The Letters of Richard P. Feynman*, Basic Books, 2005.

Bibliography

Fishbach, Ayelet and Choi, Jinhee, 'When Thinking About Goals Undermines Goal Pursuit', in *Organizational Behaviour and Human Decision Processes*, July 2012, Vol. 118.

Foer, Joshua, *Moonwalking with Einstein*, Penguin, 2012.

Gabler, Neal, *Walt Disney*, Aurum Press, 2008.

Gallagher, Kelly, *Looking Beyond the Book*, Bowker Market Research, 2012.

Glaeser, Edward, *Triumph of the City*, Macmillan, 2011.

Gopnik, Alison, Meltzoff, Andrew and Kuhl, Patricia K., *The Scientist in the Crib: What Early Learning Tells Us about the Mind*, Harper, 1999.

Graham, James M., 'Self-Expansion and Flow in Couples' Momentary Experiences, *Journal of Personality and Social Psychology*, 2008, Vol. 95, No. 3.

Greenblatt, Stephen, *Will in the World*, Pimlico, 2005.

Gruber, Howard E., *Darwin on Man: A Psychological Study of Scientific Creativity*, Wildwood House, 1974.

Hart, B., and Risley T.R., 'The Early Catastrophe', *Education Review*, Vol. 77 No. 1, 2004.

Harris, Paul L., *Trusting What You're Told: How Children Learn from Others*, Harvard University Press, 2012.

Hattie, John, *Visible Learning: A Synthesis of Over 800 Meta-Analyses Relating to Achievement*, Routledge, 2009.

Hirsch, E.D., *The Knowledge Deficit*, Houghton Mifflin Harcourt, 2007.

Holmes, Linda, 'The Sad, Beautiful Fact That We're All Going to Miss Almost Everything', NPR online, 18 April 2011.

Holt, Jim, 'Smarter, Happier, More Productive', *London Review of Books*, Vol. 33 No. 5, 3 March 2011.

Huff, Toby E., *Intellectual Curiosity and the Scientific Revolution: A Global Perspective*, Cambridge University Press, 2011.

Hume, David, *Hume's Political Discourses*, Forgotten Books, 2012.

Hutchinson, Hazel, *Brief Lives: Henry James*, Hesperus Press, 2012.

Ianelli, Vincent, 'Gun and Shooting Accidents', about.com, updated 9 January 2013.

Isaacson, Walter, *Einstein: His Life and Universe*, Simon and Schuster, 2007.

Isaacson, Walter, *Steve Jobs*, Little, Brown, 2013.

Jones, Benjamin F., *Age and Great Invention*, NBER, May 2005.

Kaplan, Stephen, 'Environmental Preference in a Knowledge-Seeking, Knowledge-Using Organism', in J.H. Barkow, L. Cosmides and J. Tooby (eds.), *The Adapted Mind*, Oxford University Press, 1992.

Kashdan, Todd, *Curious? Discover the Missing Ingredient to a Fulfilling Life*, Harper, 2010.

Keeling, Richard P. and Hersh, Richard H., *We're Losing Our Minds: Rethinking American Higher Education*, Palgrave Macmillan, 2011.

Kelly, Kevin, 'A Conversation with Kevin Kelly', *Edge.org*, 7 February 2014, http://www.edge.org./conversation/the-technium

Bibliography

Keynes, John Maynard, *Keynes on the Wireless*, in Donald Moggridge (ed.) Palgrave Macmillan, 2010.

Kirby, Joe, 'Why Teaching Skills Without Knowledge Doesn't Work', 19 June 2013, http://pragmaticreform.wordpress.com/2013/06/19/skills-without-knowledge/

Klass, Perri, 'Understanding "Ba Ba Ba" as a Key to Development', *New York Times*, 11 October 2010.

Konečni, Vladimir, 'Daniel E. Berlyne: 1924-1976', *American Journal of Psychology*, 1978, Vol. 91, No. 1, pp. 133–137.

Krauss, Lawrence M., *Quantum Man: Richard Feynman's Life in Science*, W.W. Norton, 2011.

Lareau, Annette, *Unequal Childhoods: Class, Race, and Family Life* (Second Edition), University of California Press, 2011.

Lepper, Mark R., Greene, David and Nisbett, Richard E., 'Undermining Children's Interest With Extrinsic Reward; A Test of the "Overjustification" Hypothesis', *Journal of Personality and Social Psychology*, October 1973, Vol. 28 No. 1.

Levin, Diane J., *The Whys Have It: Teaching Curiosity for Effective Negotiation and Mediation*, http://www.mediate.com/articles/LevinDbl20091116a.cfm

Lewin, Tamar, 'Students Rush To Web Classes, But Profits May Be Much Later', *New York Times*, 6 January 2013.

Malhotra, Deepak and Bazerman, Max H., *Negotiation Genius*, Bantam, 2007.

Mannes, S. and Kintsch, W., 'Knowledge Organization and Text Organization', *Cognition and Instruction*, Vol. 4, 1987.

Mar, Raymond, 'The neural bases of social cognition and story comprehension', *Annual Review of Psychology*, Vol. 62, 2011.

Marquardt, Michael, *Leading with Questions: How Leaders Find the Right Solutions by Knowing What to Ask*, Jossey-Bass, 2005.

Mayer-Schonberger, Victor, and Cukier, Kenneth, *Big Data*, John Murray, 2013.

McCartney, Paul, quoted in the *Observer*, interview with Miranda Sawyer, 13 October 2013.

McChrystal, Stanley, interview in *Foreign Affairs*, March/April 2013.

McGoey, Linsey, 'The Logic of Strategic Ignorance', *British Journal of Sociology*, 2012, Vol. 63, No. 3.

McGoey, Linsey, 'Strategic unknowns: towards a sociology of ignorance', *Economy and Society*, Vol. 41, No. 1, pp. 1–16.

McInerney, Laura, 'Why Learn?', http://lauramcinerney.com/2013/04/18/on-why-i-learn/

McKee, Robert, *Story: Substance, Structure, Style, and the Principles of Screenwriting*, Methuen, 1999.

Mill, John Stuart, *Principles of Political Economy*, in Jonathan Riley (ed.) Oxford University Press, 1994.

Mills, Steve, 'The Future of Business', IBM Thought Leadership Paper, 2007.

Mitra, Sugata, 'Build a School in the Cloud', TED Talk 2013, http://www.ted.com/talks/sugata_mitra_build_a_school_in_the_cloud.html (more details of Mitra's talks and publications can be found here: http://sugatam.

wikispaces.com/SM-Resume)

Mittelstaedt, Robert, *Will Your Next Mistake Be Fatal? Avoiding the Chain of Mistakes That Can Destroy Your Organization*, Prentice Hall, 2004.

Mokyr, Joel, *The Enlightened Economy. An Economic History of Britain*, 1700–1850, Yale University Press, 2012.

Morgan, Edmund S., *Benjamin Franklin*, Yale University Press, 2002.

Morris, Ian, *Why the West Rules – for Now*, Profile, 2010.

Munger, Charlie, *A Lesson on Elementary, Worldly Wisdom as It Relates to Investment Management and Business*, USC Business School, 1994 http://ycombinator.com/munger.html

Murphy Paul, Annie, 'Enriching Your Brain Bank', 15 July 2013, http://anniemurphypaul.com/2013/07/enriching-your-brain-bank/

Murphy Paul, Annie, 'The Power of Interest', 4 November 2013, http://anniemurphypaul.com/2013/11/the-power-of-interest/

Pagel, Mark, *Wired for Culture; Origins of the Human Social Mind*, W.W. Norton, 2012.

Phelps, Edmund, *Mass Flourishing: How Grassroots Innovation Created Jobs, Challenge and Change*, Princeton University Press, 2013.

Pinker, Steven, *How the Mind Works*, Penguin, 1999.

Poincaré, Henri, 'Mathematical Creation', in *The World of Mathematics*, in James Newman (ed.) Simon and Schuster, 1958.

Posnock, Ross, *The Trial of Curiosity*, Oxford University Press, 1991.

Postrel, Virginia, 'Serendipity and Samples Can Save Barnes & Noble', bloomberg.com, 14 July 2013.

Prospect, 'Roundtable Report, Edmund Phelps on "Mass Flourishing"', 16 October 2013.

Raichlen, David A. et al., 'Calcaneus Length Determines Running Economy: Implications for Endurance Running Performance in Modern Humans and Neandertals, *Journal of Human Evolution*, Vol. 60, No. 3, March 2011.

Reich, Robert, *The Work of Nations*, Addison-Wesley, 1991.

Richardson, M., Abraham, C. and Bond, R., 'Psychological Correlates of University Students' Academic Performance: A systematic Review and Meta-analysis', *Psychological Bulletin*, 2012, Vol. 138, pp. 353–387.

Richtel, Matt, 'Wasting Time is New Divide in Digital Era', *New York Times*, 29 May 2012.

Richtel, Matt, 'Technology Changing How Students Learn, Teachers Say', *New York Times*, 1 November 2012.

Rorty, Richard, *Essays on Heidegger and Others: Philosophical Papers, Vol. 2*, Cambridge University Press, 1991.

Rothstein, Dan, *Make Just One Change*, Harvard Education Press, 2011.

Rubik, Erno, interview with George Webster, 'The Little Cube that Changed the World', CNN, 11 October 2012, http://edition.cnn.com/2012/10/10/tech/rubiks-cube-inventor

Sansone, Carol and Thoman, Dustin B., 'Interest as the Missing Motivator in Self-Regulation', *European*

Bibliography

Psychologist, 2005, Vol. 10, No. 3, pp. 175–186.

Savage-Rumbaugh, Sue, and Lewin, Roger, *Kanzi: The Ape at the Brink of the Human Mind*, Doubleday, 1994.

Schwarz, Roger, 'Increase Your Team's Curiosity', *Harvard Business Review*, 15 July 2013.

Sherman, William H., 'How To Make Anything Signify Anything', *Cabinet*, No. 40, Winter 2010/11.

Silver, Nate, interview with Walter Frick in *Harvard Business Review*, 24 September, 2013.

Silvia, Paul, *Exploring The Psychology of Interest*, Oxford University Press, 2006.

Smith, Brian C., 'Familiarization vs. Curiosity – "Curiosity Can Be dangerous."' IALEFI Control Number 12–14.

Smith, Paul, quoted in interview with *Post Magazine*, 11 November 2012.

St Augustine, *Confessions*, in R.S. Pine-Coffin (ed.), Penguin Classics, 2002.

Tanford, Charles, *Ben Franklin Stilled the Waves; An Informal History of Pouring Oil on Water*, Duke University Press, 1989.

Thiel, Peter, based on an essay version of notes on his Stanford class CS183, 'Startup', made by Blake Masters, http://blakemasters.com/post/20400301508/cs183class1

Tizard, B., and Hughes, M., *Young Children Learning*, Fontana, 1984.

Twigger, Robert, 'Master of Many Trades', *Aeon*, 4 November 2013.

Uglow, Jenny, *The Lunar Men*, Faber & Faber, 2003.

von Stumm, S., Hell, B., and Chamorro-Premuzic, T., 'The Hungry Mind: Intellectual Curiosity is the Third Pillar of Academic Performance', *Perspectives on Psychological Science*, 2011, Vol. 6, p. 574.

von Stumm, S., Furnham, and Adrian F., 'Learning Approaches: Associations with Typical Intellectual Engagement, Intelligence and the Big Five', *Personality and Individual Differences*, 2012, Vol. 53.

Wallace, David Foster, *This Is Water: Some Thoughts, Delivered on a Significant Occasions, about Living a Compassionate Life*, Little, Brown, 2009.

Wallace, David Foster, introduction to *The Best American Essays, 2007*, Mariner, 2007.

Wallas, Graham, *The Art of Thought*, Harcourt, Brace and Company, 1926.

Wang, Da-Neng et al., 'Benjamin Franklin, Philadelphia's Favorite Son, Was a Membrane Biophysicist', *Biophysical Journal*, Vol. 104, No. 2, January 2013.

Waytz, Adam, 'The Taboo Trade-Off', *Scientific American*, 9 March 2010.

Weber, R., Perkins, D., *Inventive Minds: Creativity in Technology*, OUP, 1992.

White, T.H., *The Once and Future King*, Harper Voyager, 1996.

Whoriskey, Peter, 'For Jeff Bezos, A New Frontier', *Washington Post*, 11 August 2013.

Willingham, Daniel, *Why Don't Students Like School?*, Jossey-Bass, 2009.

Wilson, Robert S. et al., 'Life-span Cognitive Activity,

Bibliography

Neuropathologic Burden and Cognitive Aging',
Neurology, Vol. 10, July 2013.

Young, James Webb, *A Technique For Producing Ideas*,
CreateSpace, 2012.

Zuckerman, Ethan, *Rewire: Digital Cosmopolitanism in the
Age of Connection*, Norton, 2013.

Index

CURIOUS

Index

Index

Index

Index

Index